T0318230

Tourism and Nationalism in Nepal

This book explores the role of tourism in the expression of nationalism in Nepal. It investigates assemblage of images, emblems, and symbols of Nepali nationhood in various touristic representations and narratives from Nepali travellers and diasporic visitors to showcase how they express nationhood and stimulate a strong sentiment of national feeling and belongingness. The book suggests that touristic settings in Nepal provide a venue for articulation of nation, first through internal ascription, that is, the construction of identity by citizens with the nation, and second, through the promotion of distinctive touristic identity through the assertion of national uniqueness and distinguishing the nation within the larger international community.

Given the recent great political changes, post-conflict nation rebuilding, and development, Nepal offers a fascinating case study on the role of tourism and nationalism. This book will be of great interest to students, scholars, and professionals working in tourism and heritage studies, sociology, anthropology, geography, political science, and area studies, as well as those interested in the study of developing societies.

Kalyan Bhandari is a Lecturer in Events, Hospitality, and Tourism at the University of the West of Scotland, UK.

Tourism and Nationalism in Nepal

A Developing Country Perspective

Kalyan Bhandari

Routledge
Taylor & Francis Group

LONDON AND NEW YORK

First published 2019 by Routledge

2 Park Square, Milton Park, Abingdon, Oxfordshire OX14 4RN

52 Vanderbilt Avenue, New York, NY 10017

Routledge is an imprint of the Taylor & Francis Group, an informa business

First issued in paperback 2020

British Library Cataloguing-in-Publication Data
A catalogue record for this book is available from the British Library

Library of Congress Cataloging-in-Publication Data
A catalog record for this book has been requested

ISBN: 978-1-138-18439-8 (hbk)
ISBN: 978-0-367-60658-9 (pbk)

Typeset in Times New Roman
by Apex CoVantage, LLC

Contents

Preface

This book is about how tourism plays a part in the expression of national-ism in Nepal. It argues that various symbols, icons, and markers of identity in tourism help in the articulation of collective identity, which facilitates in two ways: first in the promotion of distinctive touristic identity through the assertion of national uniqueness within the larger international community and second in internal ascription, that is, the construction of identity by citizens with regard to the nation. Thus, the book provides a commentary on the development of Nepali national identity in recent history and investi-gates some current representations in tourism to see how they have narrated markers of national identity. The book also provides narratives from Nepali travellers and diasporic visitors about tourism heritage and home nation to showcase how the narratives provide a strong sentiment of national feeling and belongingness.

My interest in the idea of nationhood in touristic representation goes back to my formative years in Nepal. In 1999, I joined the newly formed Nepal Tourism Board (NTB) in Kathmandu as part of a first batch of staff. Having come from an industrial town from Nepal's southern plains that specialised in manufacturing industries, tourism was new to me, as tourism in Nepal is mainly about Western travellers trekking in the Himalayan mountains in the northern region of the country. At the first staff meeting of NTB, the chief executive officer instructed us that the NTB is a national institution and that it has national responsibility to diversify tourism across the country. He stated that the NTB should not be biased towards one culture, one religion, or one region in promoting Nepal. However, after a few weeks, when I was prepar-ing for my first trip to represent the NTB in a travel trade show abroad, my manager, who had spent a large part of her life outside Nepal, handed me a variety of promotional materials and decorative items for the Nepal stand. These items included posters and postcards of the Himalayas and its people, Buddhist prayer flags and *Jhallers*, and Thangka paintings amongst other things. None of them depicted the region I come from and things that I could easily identify myself with. I was also strictly instructed to display the pictures of the then-king and queen at the NTB's stand and wear Nepali national dress, the *Daura Suruwal*, and *Topi* throughout the show.

The way just described of narrating Nepal was different from the way I had 'experienced' and understood Nepal as one of its citizens. In the next few months, I began to readjust my imagination of Nepal and started associating with the icons and imagery of Nepal produced in the narrative of tourism. The strong contradiction between my sense of belongingness to Nepal's southern plains and the imagery of Nepal in touristic representation, which is dominated by cultural representations from the northern regions that I was exposed to after joining the NTB, sowed the seed of enquiry into the way a nation is narrated in tourism. In 2007, when I came to Scotland for my studies, the expression of 'nation' in touristic representations was my obvious choice, and since then most of my research has remained within this theme. This book is the continuation of the exploration of that theme.

The book is a result of more than a decade of curiosity about the above theme, parts of which have been previously published in various academic outlets. Thus, some of the material presented in this book has been published in the following form: 'Understanding Nepali Nationalism' in *Studies on Ethnicity and Nationalism*, 16(3) (2016); 'Imagining the Nepali "nation" through Tourism' in *Journal of Heritage Tourism*, 7(3) (2012) with Taptika Bhandari, and 'Travelling at Special Times: The Nepali Diaspora's Yearning for Belongingness' in *Tourism and Memories of Home* edited by S. Marshall, published by Channel View Publishers (2017). I would like to thank the above co-author and the publishers for allowing me to use parts of these publications in this book.

There are number of other people to whom I owe a huge thank-you for their help in completing this book. First among them are all my participants for agreeing to take part in the interviews and providing additional information and sources whenever I needed them. My former colleagues at the NTB were very forthcoming in providing anything I asked for, ranging from research support to logistics while on fieldwork in Nepal. Especially I would like to thank the chief executive officer of the NTB, Deepak Raj Joshi, for his continuous help and support. I would also like to thank Aditya Baral for his encouragement and providing feedback and comments on my draft manuscripts. Similarly, Shradha Shrestha for allowing me to use her Facebook posts and comments that I have sourced in this book. In Scotland, I would like to thank my colleagues at the University of the West of Scotland School of Business and Enterprise. I would like to thank Mary MacIlwraith for proofreading the manuscripts and my wife Taptika for painstakingly reading the first draft of each chapter and preparing the index. Finally, I thank my two sons, Nishad and Aarabh, for sacrificing their holidays to allow me to complete this book.

After I started writing the book I received a few funded projects that provided me with opportunities to travel to Nepal. I wanted to use those visits to update my information and collect the latest data for the book. In this instance, the book has greatly benefitted from the funding from the British Academy/Leverhulme Small Research Grants – SRG 2015–16. Last but not least, my very special thanks goes to my publisher, especially Faye Leerink, commissioning editor, and Ruth Anderson, editorial assistant, for their help, support, and encouragement, and especially to Ruth for her patience and understanding, as the book took a longer time to complete than expected.

Kalyan
August 2018

1 Introduction

This book examines the interface between tourism and nationalism in Nepal. It investigates how tourism provides a stage to showcase Nepal's national identity and helps in the expression of nationalism. Scholars have argued that tourists' practices do not only involve the purchase of specific goods and services, but, through touristic representations, tourism produces a way of viewing a destination. They suggest that a perception produced in tourism can play a significant role in the evolution of the viewing of a place or producing a distinctive narrative of a nation: for example, the use of symbols, artefacts, icons, and imagery, through which both visitors and natives are reminded of the heritage and cultural kinship of a nation. This book is about this role of tourism and illustrates the articulation of nationhood and nationalism in touristic settings in Nepal.

Tourism is a product of a middle-class consciousness of modern society and the sociocultural differentiation created by it (MacCannell, 1999; Urry, 2006). According to this view, the desire for tourism primarily originates from the curiosity of seeing another culture, people, and place; and the touristic consciousness is motivated by this desire for authentic experiences (MacCannell, 1999). For this reason, people as tourists travel to places different from those encountered in their everyday life, and the social, historical, cultural, and natural elements of the place they travel to are organised into a stream of impressions. These impressions help make tourism activity more than an isolated incident of just a tour or a visit to a place but rather a composite imagination of the place they travel to. In a sense, tourist attractions become a cultural experience of the society they represent and embody a discourse that reflects social meanings, relations, and entities to express nation and nationalism.

At the same time these attractions can mean different things to domestic tourists and other travellers who share their cultural identity or familial belonging with the destination. Unlike for foreign tourists who are driven by a desire to visit and know new and interesting people and their pasts, the travel aspirations of the domestic or diasporic visitors originate in the search for familiarisation and identification with others (Bhandari, 2016). For them, travel becomes associated with the individual quest for identity and self-realisation, and experiences become highly individual, subjectively interpreted, intangible, and ephemeral. For this reason some scholars have regarded tourism practices and the ways in which they are imagined and enacted as central to the construction of the self (Desforges, 2000, p. 930). According to Giddens (1991) self-identity is not something that is given but is something that is routinely 'created and sustained in the reflexive activities of the individual' (p. 52), and for travellers who have a close cultural affinity with the destination or the attraction, tourism can become one of the media for such reflexive activity to connect and identify with their nation.

In the case of Nepal, tourism has played an instrumental role in the early development and articulation of its identity and the positioning of Nepal as a unique nation in the world. This happened through the use of the Himalayas and the selective cultural representations that relied on the imagery of ethnic groups that complemented the Himalayan narrative. Such narrative was dictated partly by commercial necessity because the Western travellers expected exotic and out-of-the-ordinary accounts (Urry, 2006; Riggins, 1997), though in doing so it denied the narrative that contradicted this image. Projecting such an image was largely a political project of the Monarchical regime because creating Nepal's uniqueness strongly supported the model of Himalayan Shangri-La, in which the monarch was cast as a fulcrum of Nepali culture and society. It defined Nepali national identity through the cultural traits of the hill and mountain regions and the representations of Nepal that did not comply with this image of Nepal were not given enough attention. In this book I will show that despite huge change in the political landscape of the country, the touristic image of Nepal still relies on the Western-created image, and to a great extent there is a continuity of the agenda of constructing a singular Nepali 'national identity' and representing a particular 'version' of nationalism.

However, I also look into other ways of exchange between tourism and nationalism and a national and a personal level. The case of Lumbini discusses that heritage monuments and sites constitute repositories of national identity that make the site a resource for the articulation of national imagination. At a national level, a strong opposition to the development project at Lumbini proposed by a Chinese firm highlights the collaboration between tourism and Nepali nationalism in defending the 'perceived' invasion into its '(inter)national' heritage. At a personal level, the book discusses how a visit to a heritage attraction or a travel to one's home nation helps in making emotional connections to their nation and in reminding them of their common heritage and cultural identity. Visitors at the Buddhist heritage site in

Lumbini find themselves exalted by happiness, honour, and sense of pride while experiencing the Buddhist heritage. Same with the diasporic visitors who demonstrate that travelling to Nepal is a way through which they reconnect their association with Nepal and reaffirm their allegiance with the Nepali nation.

I must clarify here that nationalism in the book refers to the 'ideological movement for attaining and maintaining autonomy, unity and identity on behalf of a population deemed by some of its members to constitute an actual or potential nation' (Smith, 1991, p. 73). Thus, the main quest in this study is to examine tourism activities that are geared towards affirming the above characters of the Nepali nation. Such activities are driven by nationalist doctrine that contains three fundamental propositions: (a) the world is divided into nations, and each nation has its own culture, history, and destiny that make it unique among other nations; (b) nations must be united, autonomous, and free to pursue their goals; and (c) each individual belongs to a nation and that allegiance to the nation overrides all other loyalties (Triandafyllidou, 1998). The discussions in this book are mainly focussed on examining how tourism complements those nationalist doctrines through the use of various symbols, icons, images, texts, and the experience of Nepali travellers and their reflections. In another way, the book illustrates how narratives of the nation produced through the medium of tourism articulates the above principles.

In recent years, there have been some interesting studies into the role of tourism in articulating nation, nationalism, and national identity (Frew and White, 2011; Pretes, 2003; Pitchford, 2006; Park, 2010). These studies have shown that national identity and tourism intersect, overlap, and traverse, providing an opportunity for authorities to capture the imagination of tourists by referring to various aspects of national identity (Frew and White, 2011). Frew and White (2011) take the view that the connection between tourism and national identity is apparent via the promotional activities of tourism authorities. They recognise a need to better understand the multifaceted and complex connections between people and places and argue for the development of national identity-related products, though this can be debated, because in many cases national identity is a source of aggression. According to Hobsbawm (1999), nationalism by definition excludes 'all who do not belong to its own nation, that is, the vast majority of the human race' (p. 169). Thus, deliberately having products that boast of national pride can be highly political in nature and can create uneasiness in some types of visitors, especially if they are not part of that heritage or if they are from a former imperialist power.

There are numerous other studies which have shown such a 'nationalist' role played by tourism in various contexts. Pitchford (2006) has shown that tourists who visit Wales are exposed to almost every piece of the national story in some form, for example, through museums and other attractions that focus on a group's history and culture. It serves as a medium to project ethnic and nationalist messages and helps to build a revalued collective identity. In another study of Wales, Pritchard and Morgan (2001) argue that the influence of both repressive and liberating historical, political, and cultural discourse is importantly enshrined in tourism representations. In the Scottish case, McLean and Cooke (2003) have shown how heritage visitors to the National Museum of Scotland actively identify through their gaze, constructing multifarious meanings of national identity that are dynamic rather than static. However, most of these studies are based on European experiences, and a study of such a role of tourism in a non-Western context would be a helpful addition to scholarship.

In the above context, this study of the articulation and expression of Nepali nationhood in tourism has a contemporary relevance. Nepal has witnessed some of the biggest political changes in its history in recent years. Nepal experienced a huge constitutional change in 1990, when a parliamentary democracy was restored and its ethnic diversity was embraced after three decades. This was followed by an even bigger political change in 2008, when it abandoned the traditional Hindu monarchy and adopted a federal republican state. This brought about a huge change in 'national' identity and the way the Nepali nation is imagined. Hutchinson (2001) writes that state modernisation ignites competing ethnic traditions with their different versions of community, and it is important for nationalists to legitimise both traditionalism and innovation. This has been strongly witnessed in Nepal in recent years. There has been strong demand for forging a new national identity based on pluralist ideology because many of the older references to Nepali identity have outlived their purpose. This is reflected in the emergence of various 'sub-national' movements demanding due recognition of their vernacular identity in Nepal. Studies examining the discourse of the Nepali nation produced in alternative narratives, such as that of tourism, have not received enough attention in current scholarship.

There are other reasons for choosing Nepal. With the preliminary estimate of one million international visitors in 2017, tourism in Nepal is poised to become the most important feature of Nepal's sociocultural life. Rojek (2006) contends that leisure and consumption are conflated in modern life experience, which in the case of Nepal was strengthened with the implementation of neo-liberal economic policies in the early 1990s and the growth of a service economy. There were also other contributing factors for the growth of tourism: for instance, the end of decade-long internal conflict and relatively improved political stability and the recognition from all quarters of the importance of tourism for Nepal's socio-economic development.

Additionally, other influences such as globalisation and access to media and communication have brought about a huge change in the values, practices, and organisation of Nepali tourism. As a result there has been a remarkable increase in the number of domestic Nepali visitors. It is estimated that about 4 million Nepalis visited various 'home' attractions in 2017 (Dhakal, 2018). Since there were alone more than 1 million home visitors to Lumbini, the birthplace of Lord Buddha, the above estimate of domestic Nepali travellers is reasonable.

Interestingly, sociological studies on tourism in Nepal are still emerging. Some interesting studies are focussed on investigating the touristic phenomenon of the 1970s and Nepal's golden 'hippy' era. For example, there are a number of studies by Liechty, who has investigated the growth and expansion of tourism during the 1970s, specially focussing on the hippy culture and its influence in the society and culture of Kathmandu (Liechty, 2005, 2017). More recently, Linder (2017) has investigated the growth of Thamel and argues how tourism has suppressed the other narratives of Thamel and underlying contestation over its cultural significance. There are very few studies looking into the implications of the end of monarchical rule and the Hindu religion in tourism. In one study on Narayanhiti Palace Museum, Whitmarsh (2017) shows how the conversion of an erstwhile palace marks the transition of Nepal from a monarchy to a republic. She argues that the opening of the museum 'is a particular instance of the reconstruction of a Nepali national identity' (Whitmarsh, 2017, p. 89). Considering the changed socio-political context after the 1990s and the recent introduction of a new constitution in 2015, more studies on the implications of changed national context on various aspects of Nepali society and culture through their own respective disciplinary platforms would be highly relevant. This book is intended to fill this gap.

Brief outline of tourism in Nepal

However, it is important to first outline the growth and scope of tourism in Nepal. Tourism has received much attention in Nepal since it was recognised as an important moneymaking sector. Interest started after the successful ascent of Mt. Everest in 1953 that gave Nepal unprecedented media attention all over the world and helped raise the country's tourism potential. The Coronation of the then-King Mahendra, in May 1956, further added to the international exposure of Nepal, with more than 60 foreign correspondents covering the event. Tourism infrastructure was improved, with the construction of hotels for accommodating dignitaries, guests, and journalists to this event. Tourism was included in the First Development Plan (1956–1961), a document that mentioned the 'travel profession' as an important tool for 'popularising' Nepal and earning foreign currency (Chand, 2000). The government followed this with the creation of the National Tourist Development Board (NTDB) and also created the Department for Tourism, together with the Hotel and Tourism Training Center. The institutionalisation of tourism began in 1962, when the government started to keep records of incoming visitors, which stood at 6000 that year. Various measures were taken to develop tourism during the Second Development Plan (1962–65), for example, increasing tourism investments with better provisions of loans and the diversification of tourism to other areas like Pokhara and Chitwan, and airports were built in many parts of the country. This was followed up with the publication of promotional booklets and documentaries, a survey of tourism products, the setting up of tourism information centres, and the establishment of training centres for producing a middle-term labour force (see Chand, 2000).

In 1990 a significant political change took place, and Nepal adopted a constitutional monarchy, ending three decades of the old autocratic regime of the absolute monarchy. The new system was also instrumental in fully adopting an open-market economic policy and liberalisation. Tourism was one of the several industries for which state protection was lifted. With orientation towards the market economy, significant changes occurred in tourism with a new Tourism Policy in 1995 that laid a strong emphasis on the role of the private sector in tourism, development of village tourism, introduction of quality-control mechanisms, and maintenance of a regional balance while developing new tourism areas; added to this was the integration of tourism with other compatible sectors such as agriculture and cottage industries with a view to increase the length of stay, especially of Indian tourists. The year 1998 was officially promoted as Visit Nepal Year '98 and was marked throughout the year with various promotional and other events. The campaign also encouraged foreign investment in the tourism sector, and as a result, foreign investment was attracted for infrastructure projects, primarily hotel and resort developments. The new tourism policy also recognised a need for an autonomous body for tourism marketing.

During the entire 1990s, the operation of tourism remained largely in the hands of private-sector tourism entrepreneurs. Restriction was lifted for operating travel agencies and trekking agencies. Foreign investment in the tourism infrastructures was welcomed, although no foreign investment in travel agencies or trekking agencies was permitted. Only registered guides were allowed to carry out sightseeing activities. Most of the areas of the country were opened for tourists, with few exceptions pertaining to the so-called restricted areas, for which a special entrance permit was required. In 1999, Nepal Tourism Board was established, and since then marketing and promotion of tourism are taken care of by it. The Board has been carrying out promotional activities in the selected target markets, involving the private sector in all its marketing activities. Besides marketing and promotion, the Board now is also responsible for the improvement of existing products and development of new ones in order to diversify tourism activities in the country.

Tourism remained relatively smooth until 1999, the year that saw half a million visitors. But the political turmoil triggered by the violent revolution led by the Maoist party in 1996 gradually started to take its toll on tourism, with the result that the number of visitors in 2002 fell to the level of 1990 (Bhattarai, Conway and Shrestha, 2005). Following the increased Maoist insurgency, in 2002 the king staged a coup d'état and started direct rule in various forms. In 2006 Nepal's democratic forces joined hands with the Maoists, in reaction to the king's coup, which successfully obliged the king to give up his powers, which remained suspended until the elected constitution assembly in 2008 formally ended the institution of monarchy. Tourism has seen positive growth since then.

The main areas of tourist interest remain Kathmandu for cultural tourism, Pokhara, Annapurna circuit treks, the Everest region for adventure tourism, and Chitwan, a popular destination for Jungle safaris, for nature tourism. Trekking and mountaineering forms a major reason for Western visitors to travel to Nepal. For Indian visitors, business and Hindu religious pilgrimage remain the main attractions that are highly confined within Kathmandu and its peripheral regions. According to the Ministry of Culture, Tourism, and Civil Aviation, the gross foreign exchange earnings in the convertible currency from tourism in the year 2016 stood at US $518.5 million, and tourist expenditure stood at US $53 per day (MoTCA, 2016). India is the biggest tourist contributor to Nepal, contributing about 16% of total visitors. The proportion of Indian visitors, which used to be more than one-third of total visitors, has significantly come down in the last decade. This is followed by China, which accounts for about 14% of total arrivals. There has been a huge improvement in the Chinese market in the last decade, from 5.2% in 2007. The major tourist-generating countries are Sri Lanka (7.6%), USA (7.1%), UK (6.1%), and Japan, Germany, and France, with each representing around 3%. The principal reasons for visits are holiday (50%), pilgrimage (13%), and trekking and mountaineering (12%). Tourism is highly seasonal and is spread around February–April and September–November.

According to the World Travel and Tourism Council (WTTC, 2015), the direct contribution of tourism to Nepal's GDP in 2014 was 4.3%. This primarily reflects the economic activity generated by industries such as hotels, travel agents, airlines, and other passenger transportation services and includes the activities of the restaurant and leisure industries directly supported by tourism. This contribution is expected to grow to 4.4% by 2025.

Tourism generated half a million jobs in 2014 and is expected to grow at a yearly rate of 3.0% over the next ten years. However, it was estimated that the above targets for Nepal were likely to be affected because of the deadly earthquake of April 2015. The quake damaged many of its UNESCO-listed World Heritage Sites and some trekking routes, and as a result, according to the Department of Immigration, the total arrivals in 2015 fell to a six-year low of just over half a million (TKP, 2016). Interestingly, Nepal has made a remarkable recovery in tourism, and the number of tourist arrivals nearly touched the one million mark in 2017, less than three years after the earthquake.

Methodology

This book takes the social constructivist approach to research. Social constructivists emphasise the making of knowledge by communities of individuals rather than by individuals (Watkins, 2000). According to Watkins (2000), knowledge is viewed as a collaborative intersubjective construction and is appropriated by individuals from the socially organised practices of the group in which they participate (Cobb, 1994). Thus, the meaning of nation, nationhood, and national identity is understood as embedded in participatory forms of social practice among the Nepali people, and it is subject to the structuring influences of historical processes and sociocultural beliefs that surround these practices. Differences in meaning of these concepts are subsequently held to represent variations in social practice and reflect different normative beliefs held by different groups. Similarly, the changes in meaning are associated with evolving social practices and indicate increasing individual enculturation in these practices.

This book is a result of the various sources of data collected over the period of the last eight years. Ten visits were made to Nepal between 2010 and 2018, and I visited tourist attractions, sightseeing places, museums, and heritage centres and public and private tourism agencies. The book relies on both obtrusive and unobtrusive data such as 'texts' or 'artifacts' (Hesse-Biber and Leavy, 2006). I examined unobtrusive data, for example, promotional materials, brochures, and CD ROMs, websites, Facebook, and other social media sites of tourism agencies and businesses along with museum displays, souvenir, and other promotional tools. An important aspect of this type of data is that it exists independently of research, that is, the data are not influenced through research interaction and are 'naturalistic' (Hesse-Biber and Leavy, 2006).

Additionally, unstructured interviews were carried out with a sample of more than 45 individuals in total. They can be categorised under three groups. The first groups were those associated with the tourism and leisure industry. They included staff at the Nepal Tourism Board and Executive Committee members; members of Nepali diasporic communities; tourism consultants; museum and heritage centre staff members; academics; journalists and media commentators; tourism industry professionals; tourism policy makers from the Ministry of Tourism, Culture, and Civil Aviation and the Tourism and External Affairs Ministry among others. A total of 18 interviews were carried out with this group, and the questions centred on aspects of tourism in Nepal; heritage; the impact of earthquake; the ethnographic museum and its artefacts; purpose and production process of tourism promotional media; and other aspects of Nepal's tourism representation and imagery. The interview participants were identified from the researcher's own long engagement with Nepal and were purposefully chosen because they were 'information-rich' actors on account of their positions, involvement in key policy processes, and reputations as influential and 'informed' insiders (Bramwell and Meyer, 2007). In some cases participants were also chosen based on information from the media and other documents and from snowball suggestions made by respondents who were contacted during the early stages of writing this book.

The second sample of interviewees included 12 individuals from the Nepali diaspora who visited Nepal after the earthquake in April 2015. The diasporic visitors were interviewed during their visits in Nepal, and some were later followed up after their visit in the UK. The third groups were 15 Nepali visitors at various tourism attractions and most prominently with domestic visitors at the Lumbini heritage site on two occasions in July 2016 and May 2018. The interviews focussed on their perception of Lumbini, the place of Lumbini in their national imagination, and the role of the visit in their self-identification. Various books and other literature written on Nepal and the Nepali cultural world were widely consulted throughout the data collection and interpretation stages.

The structure of the book

The book is structured as follows. In Chapter 2, I will critically assess the development and shaping of a distinctive national narrative of Nepal and try to examine how tourism fitted itself within this account. In order to understand the deeper relationships between tourism and national identity, it is imperative to consider the processes and ideologies that have contributed to the formation of the present tourism imagery and destination identity. Thus, I will outline the discourse of Nepali national identity in recent history and assess how tourism has become intersected with and companion to this narrative. Chapter 3 examines the representation of Nepal in some tourism media and argues that such representations provide a platform to articulate national identity and express nationalism. The chapter cautions that national character in tourism representations can be staged and contrived and does not necessarily exemplify an authentic version of the nation, preventing tourism from playing a meaningful role in bringing in more 'sub-national' identities into the composite imagery of Nepal.

Chapter 4 explores the intricacies of heritage at a World Heritage site and illustrates how touristic heritage can become the repository of national consciousness and can evoke a strong nationalist sentiment. The chapter argues that the agency of national actors in Lumbini is informed by power struggle or claim over heritage, which is the result of perceived threat to the Lumbini heritage. Chapter 5 looks into the identification of the Nepal diaspora with the Nepali nationhood after the April 2015 earthquake. It discusses the articulation of root, identity, and belonging in the context of Nepali diasporic communities in the UK and argues that the earthquake enabled them to reconnect and negotiate their bonding with and the sense of belonging to the Nepali nation. Finally, Chapter 6 presents the summary of the discussions in the chapters and provides some reflections on the future interaction of tourism with nationalism.

References

Bhandari, K. (2016). Imagining the Scottish Nation: Tourism and Homeland Nationalism in Scotland. *Current Issues in Tourism*, 19(9), 913–929. DOI: 10.1080/13683500.2013.789005.

Bhattarai, K., Conway, D. and Shrestha, N. (2005). Tourism, Terrorism and Turmoil in Nepal. *Annals of Tourism Research*, 32(3), 669–688.

Bramwell, B. and Meyer, D. (2007). Power and Tourism Policy Relations in Transition. *Annals of Tourism Research*, 34(3), 766–788.

Chand, D. (2000). *Nepal's Tourism Uncensored Facts*. Varanasi: Pilgrims Publishing.

Cobb. P. (1994). Where Is the Mind? Constructivist and Socio-Cultural Perspectives on Mathematical Development. *Educational Researcher*, 23(7), 13–20.

Desforges, L. (2000). Traveling the World: Identity and Travel Biography. *Annals of Tourism Research*, 24(4), 926–945.

Dhakal, Y. (2018). Fastaudai Tourism (Tourism Growing). *Naya Patrika* Online. Available at: www.nayapatrikadaily.com/2018/08/11/81569/ (accessed 14 August 2018).

Frew, E. and White, L. (2011). *Tourism and National Identities: An International Perspective*. London: Routledge.

Giddens, A. (1991). *Modernity and Self-Identity: Self and Society in the Late Modern Age*. Cambridge: Polity Press.

Hesse-Biber, S. N. and Leavy, P. (2006). *The Practice of Qualitative Research*. London: Sage Publications.

Hobsbawm, E. (1999). *Nations and Nationalism since 1780*. Cambridge: Cambridge University Press.

Hutchinson, J. (2001). Nations and Culture. In M. Guibernau and J. Hutchison (Eds.), *Understanding Nationalism* (pp. 74–96). Cambridge: Polity Press.

The Kathmandu Post (TKP). (2016). Arrivals Hit 6-Year Low as Quake, Agitation Take Toll. Available at: http://bit.ly/20ib9KPhttp://kathmandupost.ekantipur.com/news/2016-01-22/arrivals-hit-6-year-low-as-quake-agitation-take-toll.html.

Liechty, M. (2005). Building the Road to Kathmandu: Notes on the History of Tourism in Nepal. *Himalaya, the Journal of the Association for Nepal and Himalayan Studies*, 25(1), 19–28.

Liechty, M. (2017). *Far Out: Countercultural Seekers and the Tourist Encounter in Nepal*. Chicago: University of Chicago Press.

Linder, B. (2017). Of 'Tourist' Places: The Cultural Politics of Narrating Space in Thamel. *Himalaya, the Journal of the Association for Nepal and Himalayan Studies*, 37(1), 41–56.

MacCannell, D. (1999). *The Tourist a New Theory of the Leisure Class*. Berkeley, CA: University of California Press.

Maguire, S. (2006). Brother Jonathan and John Bell a Nation: The transactional nature of American nationalism in the early Nineteenth century. *National Identities*, 18(2), 179–198.

McLean, F. and Cooke, S. (2003). Constructing the Identity of a Nation: The Tourist Gaze at the Museum of Scotland. *Tourism Culture and Communication*, 4(3), 153–162.

Ministry of Culture, Tourism and Civil Aviation (MoTCA). (2016). *Nepal Tourism Statistics (2016)*. Kathmandu: Government of Nepal.

Park, H. (2010). Heritage Tourism: Emotional Journeys to Nationhood. *Annals of Tourism Research*, 37(1), 116–135.

Pitchford, S. (2006). Identity Tourism: A Medium for Native American Stories. *Tourism Culture and Communication*, 6(2), 85–105.

Pretes, M. (2003). Tourism and Nationalism. *Annals of Tourism Research*, 30(1), 125–142.

Pritchard, A. and Morgan, N. J. (2001). Culture Identity and Tourism Representation: Marketing Cymru or Wales? *Tourism Management*, 22(2), 167–179.

Riggins, S. H. (1997). *The Language and Politics of Exclusion: Others in Discourse*. London: Sage Publications.

Rojek, C. (2006). Leisure and Consumption. *Leisure/Losir*, 30(1), 475–486.

Smith, A. D. (1991). *National Identity*. London: Penguin.

Triandafyllidou, A. (1998). National Identity and the 'Other'. *Ethnic and Racial Studies*, 21(4), 593–612.

Urry, J. (2006). *The Tourist Gaze*. London: Sage Publications.

Watkins, M. (2000). Ways of Learning about Leisure Meaning. *Leisure Sciences*, 22, 93–107.

Whitmarsh, B. (2017). Staging Memories at the Narayanhiti Palace Museum, Kathmandu. *Himalaya, the Journal of the Association for Nepal and Himalayan Studies*, 37(1), 84–97.

World Travel and Tourism Council (WTTC). (2015). *Travel and Tourism Economic Impact 2015 Nepal*. Available at: www.wttc.org//media/files/reports/economic%20impact%20research/countries%202015/nepal2015.pdf.

2 Nation, nationalism, and tourism in Nepal

This chapter provides background on the development of Nepali national identity in recent history and its appearance in tourism representations. The assessment of the past is helpful in understanding what our predecessors have constructed for us and can provide insights on the most potent elements in the construction of nationalism. Those who approach nationalism from historical perspectives take the view that history is an inevitable prerequisite for nationalism (Smith, 1991; Gellner, 1983; Anderson, 1991; Hobsbawm and Ranger, 1983): history provides a necessary ingredient for nationalism to foster. According to them, history is important in the formation of identity because 'historic territory and historical memories' are important features of the concept of the nation (Smith, 1991; Ashworth, 1994). My argument in this chapter does not deal with the historicity of Nepali national identity, but I will critically assess the development and shaping of a distinctive national narrative of Nepal and try to examine how tourism fitted itself within this account.

Hobsbawm (1983) believes that a national phenomenon cannot be understood without careful investigation of recent symbols or suitable tailored discourse such as 'national history', which every modern nation constructs to assert continuity with the appropriate historic past. Ashworth (1998) has extended this idea to the context of heritage tourism and shown how heritage tourism sites can become an important catalyst in amplifying and projecting such national iconography. In this role, tourism tends to give a new identity to a place selected from those easily recognisable, reproducible, and sellable components of the place identity and which it simplifies, homogenises, and stereotypes (Ashworth, 1998). It is usually actors in tourism who are inclined to stress the tradition and historical continuity of a particular place. According to Rose (1995), this is where tourism is linked to nationalism. In the case of Nepal, such a role for tourism was fully explored by agencies, and tourism was employed to provide a 'desired' narrative of the nation. This chapter will first provide a commentary on polity that dominated the 'national' narrative of 'Nepaliness' or 'Nepali identity' in recent history, and then it will illustrate how tourism became intersected with and companion to this 'national' narrative.

Understanding nations and nationalism

The concept of 'nation' has been explained in a variety of ways. The study of 'nation' and nationalism can be divided into two important paradigms that dominate scholarship: (a) the primordialist approach that supposes that 'nation' is a primordial category, or one founded upon primordial attachments and (b) the modernist approach that supposes 'nation' to be a modern ideology and movement. There are different variants of both of these approaches. Some primordialists believe that ethnic ties and nationalisms are derived from individual reproductive drives, which find their expression in 'nepotistic' behaviour in order to maximise their inclusive fitness (Van den Berghe, 1995). For other primordialists the cultural 'givens' of kinship, language, religion, race, and territory provide foci for overriding attachments (Shils, 1957; Geertz, 1973). However, Smith (2000) believes there are two principal flaws in the primordialist approach: (a) they fail to explain how we extrapolate from small kin groups to the much larger and extended communities of ethnie or nation and (b) they neglect the considerable social and cultural changes that transform the character of the communities which coalesce around them.

In opposition to the primordialists, the modernist paradigm puts forward a more compelling approach to the nation. Modernist explanations have several forms that come associated with the basic idea of modernism: for example sociocultural, economic, political, ideological, and constructionist. The most vocal scholar to propound the modernist approach is Ernest Gellner, who in his 1964 book *Thought and Change* outlined the new theory of nationalism that focussed on the effect of uneven global modernisation and argued that nationalism is a product of industrial society, triggered by the spread of education. Tom Nairn (1981) has further developed Gellner's theory to argue that the uneven development of capitalism caused by imperialism stimulates nationalism. In contrast to Gellner's idea that demands cultural homogeneity, Nairn's idea is based on heterogeneity: it appeals to the people as a whole and identifies the nation with the people.

However, Hobsbawm (1999) challenges the basic premises of Gellner and Nairn by arguing that urbanisation and industrialisation undermine the condition that breeds ethnically, culturally, and linguistically homogeneous groups' desire for nationalism. Nairn and Gellner's economic theory of nationalism can also be challenged because they lay too much emphasis on economic factors and ignore sociocultural conditions. Nationalism can flourish in all kinds of economic milieux: among rich and poor populations, in stagnant and mobile societies, and in backward and advanced regions (Smith, 2000). Thus, Smith (2000) considers that rather than economic or social discontent, it is the ethnic and cultural ties on which a claim to nationalism is based. For Smith (1991, pp. 14–15), the nation signifies a cultural and political bond, uniting in a single political community of all who share an historic culture and homeland. Nonetheless, one important flaw in his approach is the question of how a large entity like 'nation' would be based on ethnic bonding and how one can explain the existence of many 'multinational' nations, for example, India.

The above question equally applies to Nepal. According to the 2011 census there are a total of 64 ethnic and 58 caste groups in Nepal (Sharma, 2012), and there is great cultural division within a single group as well. Although ethnicity invokes a sense of rootedness and ancient origins, the existence of many ethnic groups also displays competing conceptions of descent, history, culture, and territory (Hutchinson, 2001, p. 83). As such the modernists' proclivity to view nations as culturally homogenous and culture as 'value free' (Hutchinson, 2001, p. 83) is not well founded and does not provide a full answer to the question of what binds a nation together – especially for a multi-ethnic country like Nepal.

If we are to consider the relationship between nations and ethnic groups, we must focus on some more essential process, which is the spontaneous construction of ethnic identities as a result of group interaction, a phenomenon which obviously occurs in both the modern and pre-modern worlds (Conversi, 1995). Barth (1981) provides some important insights into this process. He takes the view that ethnic distinctions are maintained and asserted through interaction and interdependence. According to him, ethnic groups are categories of ascription and identification by the actors themselves, and the nature and continuity of their self-identity depends on the maintenance of a boundary with the 'Other' or the outsider. According to him, the cultural feature that signals the boundary may change over time and with greater interaction and exposure, the cultural characteristics of the members may likewise be transformed; however, there is always a boundary between members and outsiders.

Conversi (1995, p. 77) calls this approach *transactionalism* and advances the point that 'nationalism is both a process of border maintenance and creation'. It focuses on human transactions and believes that all forms of interaction need norms and regulations, and borders represent the core of such regulations (Conversi, 1995). It argues that borders are essential to all human processes, at both the individual and the social levels, and all processes of identity construction are simultaneously border generating and border deriving. The approach appreciates the role of internal ascription, i.e., the construction of identity by citizens with the nation (Smith, 2009) and also the development of the nation within the larger international community (Tilly, 2005). It delves into the construction of national identity within a particular historical context and in relation to each other (Maguire, 2015): for instance, Greenfeld (1995) notes that the definition of the nation is at least in part determined by the perceived place of the nation in relation to other nations but maintains the notion of the nation as a primarily self-defining group.

Scholars have looked into nationalism from a boundaries perspective with a variety of disciplinary positions such as social psychology, social identity, social movements, creation of inequality and class differences, and cultural practices (Breuilly, 2013; Stephens, 2013; Wimmer, 2013). Most of these have applied the approach as part of nation building, examining the effects of decolonisation or unmaking of borders on the construction of national identity (see Jackson and Molokotos-Leiderman, 2014 for detailed literature on this). However, studies that see ethnicity and nationalism as tools of boundary creation or as human transactions are given less attention, and the case of Nepal is no exception.

Studies on Nepali nationalism were very limited until 1990 (Quigley, 1987; Burghart, 1984; Rose, 1971; Gaige, 1975); however, there has been a profusion of studies on the subject since then, and most of them are dominated by anthropologists and political scientists (Gellner, Czarnecka and Whelpton, 2008; Malagodi, 2008, 2013; Lawoti and Hangen, 2013; Hachhethu, 2003; Onta, 1996; Hutt, 2012; Rademacher, 2007; Chalmers, 2003). One of the most prominent post-1990 publications is an ethnographic collection which takes a long-term view of the various processes of ethnic and national development and examines the ways that different political regimes have framed and attempted to control castes and ethnic groups (Gellner, Czarnecka and Whelpton, 2008). This volume tangentially appreciates the role of boundary by dismissing the modernist presupposition that everyone has one and only one nation or one and only one ethnic attachment and recognises that people very often do have multiple and overlapping attachments, and as such they belong to one group for some purposes and other groups for different purposes (also see Gellner, 2001).

A follow-up study on the consequences of ethnic mobilisation is presented in a more recent volume by Lawoti and Hangen (2013) which examines the rapid rise in ethnic and nationalist mobilisation and conflict since 1990, the dynamics and trajectories of these movements, and their political consequences for Nepal. In the last decade the issue of Nepali nationalism has been discussed from various perspectives: for example, the debate surrounding equality or social exclusion and inclusion has strongly challenged the very premise of official Nepali nationalism (see Lawoti, 2005; Bhattachan,

2009; Giri, 2010; Gurung, Tamang and Turin, 2014). Other studies on Nepali nationalism appreciate the role of history, language, and culture in shaping how we are viewed and perceived by others. For example, Hutt (2012) argues that Nepal's adoption of a new national anthem in 2007 reflected a decision to establish a new social and political order that was republican, federal, and inclusive of the country's many minority communities.

Similarly, Malagodi (2013) examines the complex relationship between law and politics and emphasises the role of cultural identity in making institutional choices relating to the framing and implementation of the Nepali Constitution. She also analyses the patterns of legal exclusion that have resulted in the growing politicisation of identity and the current demand for state restructuring based on ethnic federalism and group rights. Though the above studies provide a good insight into the discourse of the historically transitional period and are helpful in the contextualised understanding of contemporary national narratives, they all focus on internal ascription or self-identification. They do not provide a complete picture of the formation of national identity because identities are negotiated within a particular historical context (Sahlins, 1989) and through the categorisation of a nation vis-à-vis other nations (Jenkins, 1995).

Cultural identity and boundary construction in Nepal

Nepal is one of the oldest nations in South Asia. The country was established in the mid-18th century when a king of Gorkha set out to bring together what would become present-day Nepal. For a long period of its history Nepal was in isolation and cut off from the outside world because of internal politics and restrictions imposed by British India. The formal establishment of Nepal's political status came in 1923, when the restrictions on Nepalese diplomatic relationships and trade were finally removed. Nepal's isolation during the 18th and 19th centuries has a key role to play in the construction of its current 'national' character in two ways. First, it helped the various ethnicities to keep their distinctiveness; as a result Nepal now has an extremely diverse society with more than 100 ethnic and cultural groups (Sharma, 2012). Second, this isolation also involved the exception that it was integrated into the capitalist-dominated economy of India (Blaikie, Cameron and Seddon, 1980), which had an effect on Nepal's national polity that has always been characterised by its deeply apprehensive attitudes towards India. However, Barth (1981) challenges the view that ethnic identities are developed or fostered in isolation. He argues that ethnic distinctions and cultural differences persist despite inter-ethnic contact and interdependence. The development of Nepali cultural identity is a good example, as we will see below.

A real sense of Nepali nationhood only started to evolve after the 19th century, when greater interaction began with external forces, namely India. According to Burghart (1984), the demarcation of the border between British India and Nepal in 1816 sparked the formation of the concept of nation-state in Nepal. Other important episodes that played a significant role in the development of nation-state were the designation of Nepali as the official language of Nepal (c.1930), the implicit differentiation of the monarchy from the state (c.1960), and the formation of a culturally unique polity (c.1960) (Burghart, 1984). Burghart's analysis is, however, largely concerned with Hindu concepts, values, and understanding and has been criticised for presenting nationalism as singular, unchallenged, and promoting a dominant world view (Lawoti and Hangen, 2013). However, he is correct in pointing out that the mobilisation of cultural identity in the expression of Nepali nationalism came in the second half of the 20th century. Interestingly, it did not start in Nepal, but the formation of the cultural sense of Nepal's identity was founded in India by a small group of expatriated Nepalis in British India. Onta (1996) writes, 'while Rana rulers of Nepal and their intellectual bards did not build a historical genealogy for the Nepali nation . . . the Nepali proto middle-class actors in British India did exactly that via the self-conscious fostering of the Nepali language and the writing of a *bir* (brave) history of the Nepali nation' (Onta, 1996, p. 39).

In 1960 the Nepalese king dissolved the elected parliament and introduced the *Panchayati* system, a political system founded on absolute monarchy, which played a key role in the shaping of modern Nepali national identity that was largely based on the Nepali language and hill identity. Efforts were made to create or invent a mono-cultural sense of 'Nepaliness' on the basis of its 'unique' culture that rested on the philosophy 'one nation, one language, one dress, one religion' (Subba, 2002, p. 129). Various symbols and icons were invented and aggressively employed to give a distinctive sense of Nepali national identity, and institutions were created to advance this 'nationalist' project. For instance, *Nepal Sahitya Kala Pratisthan*, later renamed as *Nepal Rajkiya Pragya Pratisthan* or 'the Royal Academy', was established under the king's chairmanship to promote the 'nation's glory' in the name of the development of literature, culture, art, and knowledge. The academy made a significant contribution in the field of Nepali literature, culture, art, and knowledge, though much of this has now been questioned by various linguistic groups.

The *Panchayati* project was despotic in character, though it did not necessarily force people to dissolve their identity. Burghart (1984) writes that the king respected the customs of different countries and registered the fact of this difference by various means. Still, the assertion of a singular Nepali identity had a far-reaching effect in forging 'Nepali' identity. Until the 18th century, there was no modern nation called Nepal. Though there was some mention of the 'Nepali' nation in some pre-historic texts, this was largely made in reference to the kingdoms of the Kathmandu valley. In the absence of a nation of Nepal, the question of the collective noun 'Nepali', representing the inhabitants of present-day Nepal, did not exist. Hamilton (1819, p. 246), who visited Nepal in 1801, noted that the nobles and soldiers of Gorkha 'despised the name Nepal'. Burghart (1984) writes that although the British referred to the Nepalese rulers as kings of Nepal, the members of the Shah Dynasty prior to the 1930s thought of themselves as being kings from Gorkha. The *Panchayati* regime institutionally recreated icons, symbols, and representations which were mostly derived from Hindu mythologies so as to represent the character of *Nepaliness or 'Nepalipan'* (Rademacher, 2007, p. 128). The regime indirectly forced individuals, groups, and communities to promote the symbols in order to become culturally Sanskritised as Nepali. This contributed to the evolutionary process of creating a distinctive *Nepali Jati* (ethnicity) and helped create Nepali ethnicity as an historical community.

The appropriateness of creating such an identity can be debated, but the invention of a collective noun or 'national' culture is not new. Smith (1986) says that nationalists 'rediscover' historical periods to legitimise their political strategies and to find lessons for the present. In fact there exists a theory of nationalism based on invented tradition. Hobsbawm (1983) provides an historical theory of nationalism that lays emphasis on manufactured historical legacy constructed through 'invented tradition'. He argues that all invented traditions use references to the past not only to cement group cohesion but also for the legitimisation of action.

Being an accomplished poet and songwriter himself, the then-Nepalese King Mahendra (1955–1972) was a cultural nationalist. The primary aim of cultural nationalists is to revive what they regard as a distinctive and primordial collective personality which has a name, unique origin, history, culture, homeland, and social and political practices (Hutchinson, 1999). Such revivals are influenced by a particular perception of the threat to its national existence by a powerful neighbour or 'the Other'. In Nepal's case this 'other' was India. Many people would take the view that the threat from India was validated by its annexation of Sikkim, a small kingdom in the Himalayas in the early 1970s (for Sikkim's annexation to India see Datta-Ray, 2013; Kazi, 1993). But it can be argued that this is not necessarily true. A Nepali psychologist has the following to say on Nepalis' perception of India five years before Sikkim was annexed to India:

Nepalis had to reckon with the Indians so long and so often that they are more prone to infer the latters' intents quickly than to observe their overt behaviour. Due to the high degree of intimacy between the two countries through the ages, whatever the Indians do in actual practice is not considered as important as what the Nepalis think the Indians mean.

(Bhuwan Lal Joshi in Rose, 1971, p. 16)

King Mahendra did try to exploit anti-India feeling and consolidate his power by infusing Nepali culture with politics and presenting himself as a saviour of Nepalis everywhere. He invited noted literati from Nepali diasporas, particularly in northeast India, to live and settle in Nepal. Such a gesture by the king was important in bringing the political and cultural dimension of Nepali identity closer. One of the strong proponents of that philosophy is the dethroned King Gyanendra. He still tries to claim the monarchy's return is necessary for the existence of the Nepali nation and questions, *'mulukai narahe hami kasari Nepali?'*, which translates into English: 'How will *we* remain (Nepali) without the existence of the Nepali nation?' (Shah, 2012). According to Pradhan (1982), the word 'Nepali' connotes three different meanings, viz. a language, a citizen of Nepal, and a cultural identity. The king's statement muddles the latter two to make a claim that the existence of a separate Nepali state is vital for the distinctive identity of Nepalis all over the world.

The choice of the word *Muluk* by the king to refer to Nepal or the country also has significance. *Muluk* has a unique connotation in the Nepali language. The Gorkha rulers, the forefathers of the Nepali kings, claimed their sovereignty by exercising proprietorial authority over their possessions (*muluk*), and ritual authority within their realm (*desa*) and various countries (also *desa* or *des*), in which the kings' tenants or subjects were natives who claimed certain rights to their land and way of life on the basis of ancestral authority (Burghart, 1984, p. 103). Each of these three concepts – possessions, realm, and country – specified a different relationship between ruler, land, and people, and each was legitimised with respect to different kinds of authority – proprietorial, ritual, and ancestral (1984, p. 103). The boundaries between the three were not always the same, and use of the term was to claim cultural propriety over greater territory. The kings, thus, often used *Muluk* to claim cultural authority not only within Nepal but also transcending the political boundary to reach people in northeast India. *Muluk* can also mean 'homeland'. The ex-king's reference can be interpreted as meaning that the absence of homeland is tantamount to the loss of Nepali identity, no matter where Nepalis live.

The *Panchayati* version of state-sponsored nationalism has received much condemnation over the last two and a half decades. However, we could also see state-sponsored nationalism from an historical perspective. With the emergence of new nations in the former colonial territories of

Asia and Europe, the idea of nation building and national integration was in vogue. The central premise was that the population of the state, or the citizenry, is progressively welded into a 'nation' in the crucible of a bounded and relatively homogenous transactional and communicative space. That space is defined and delimited by state-wide social, political, economic, and cultural institutions and processes (Brubaker, 1992, p. 80). The intervention of the *Panchayati* state created such homogeneity, and its approach was similar to the 'official nationalism' (Seton-Watson's term) of imperial governments in Europe.

In 1990, Nepal adopted a multiparty parliamentary democracy. The erstwhile state-sponsored nationalism became less relevant, and cultural homogeneity was strongly disputed. The Tibeto-Burman hill communities challenged the notion of one nation, one identity (Subba, 2002, p. 129): for a detailed commentary on the politics of ethnic identity since the mid-1990s, see Gellner, Pfaff-Czarnecka and Whelpton (2008), Shneiderman (2014), and Lecomte-Tilouine (2009). T.B. Subba (2002) endorses the view that the present crisis of Nepali national identity has to do mainly with the earlier attempt to impose a monolithic and homogenous Nepali identity on all Nepalis.

However, people's discontent with the exclusionary polity of the past was very strong, and Nepal has now adopted a policy of appeasement to address this. As a result, there are now 40 public holidays, of which 35 exist for celebrating vernacular culture in order to appreciate multiculturalism, though the majority of them are still labelled 'Khas-Arya' holidays. In Nepal 'Khas-Arya' refers to an ethno-linguistic group also known as 'Parbatiyas', who are accused of their history of socio-political dominance in Nepal. Despite having the highest number of public holidays of any country, there is no dedicated 'national' day in Nepal. Though some scholars believe that national days have no real function in a secular age, others take the view that they are commemorative devices in time and place for reinforcing national identity and cannot be overlooked altogether (McCrone and McPherson, 2009). Inability to agree on a 'national' day or a 'national culture' is disconcerting if we consider that nationalism draws on all kinds of sources – myth, legend, religion, history, art, culture, language, literature – to create a cult of the nation (Smith, 2008). However, there have been some voices raised lately to reinstate 'Prithvi Jayanti' to mark the birthday of King Prithvi Narayan Shah, who founded Nepal. Does this mean the glue that binds the Nepali nation is losing its strength? I believe it would be wrong to think so. However, the manifestation of national identity has definitely started to change. Until now I have argued that Nepali identity has been largely shaped by its long interaction with external elements and has created a distinctive identity of its own. In the following section, I will discuss how tourism has operated within the above account and how it has negotiated the articulation of Nepali national identity in touristic narratives.

Tourism and national identity in Nepal

The *transactional* approach to nationalism is very relevant in the analysis of tourism because tourism is a process that allies with the way a nation is represented to outsiders in order to construct it as 'the other'. In essence, tourism is an instrument that represents 'us' to 'them' and in doing so, it presents a destination as 'the other'. This process of self-identification vis-à-vis 'the other' often uses elements of the identity of the nation. This explanation is related to the theoretical contribution of Edward Said and his idea of Orientalism. Said (1991) considers Orientalism 'a Western style for dominating, restructuring and having authority over the Orient for managing and producing the Orient (p. 3)'. It is 'a mode of *discourse*, supporting institutions, vocabulary, scholarship, imagery, doctrines, even colonial bureaucracies and colonial styles' (p. 2). Orientalism, therefore, is an imperialist epistemology which assumes that the differences between Western and Eastern civilisations are ontological (Said, 1991). However, scholars extend this idea and believe that Orientalism is not simply the autonomous creation of the West but rather that the Orient also participates in its construction, reinforcement, and circulation (Dirlik, 1996; Ong, 1998; Zhang, 2006: all cited in Yan and Santos, 2009). This is often referred to as Self-Orientalism. Bhabha (1992, p. 438) states that 'it is from those who suffered the sentence of history – subjugation, domination, diaspora, displacement – that we learn our enduring lessons for living and thinking'. Thus, Western conceptions heavily influence the self-produced images of the Orient. Thus, Orientalist discourse cannot be approached as strictly the result of Western ideology but rather as the combination of changing Western and Eastern sociocultural and ideological conditions.

The case of Nepal is a very good example of the above observation. The tourist image of Nepal was built around the image of Shangri-La, the mythic kingdom created by James Hilton in the 1930s book of that fabled name (Hutt, 1996), and the majestic grandeur of the sacred Himalayas, which were both the creation of Western perception. Liechty (2017) argues that Nepal's development as a tourist destination was the result of the deep-seated Western longing for an imagined 'otherness'. According to him, Westerners have imagined Nepal as a land untainted by modernity and its capital, Kathmandu, as a veritable synonym of 'Oriented mystique' (Liechty, 2017, p. x). Liechty (2017) outlines the evolution of Nepali tourism within the wider context of international relations in the 1950s and argues that tourism in Nepal was an encounter between Nepal and the Western, who share a complex, historically constituted stage, and as such it played an important role in shaping Nepali identity in the modern world. He continues that touristic encounters brought about a change in the way Nepalis viewed themselves vis-à-vis a globalised world and were helpful in creating a dichotomy between 'us' and 'them' in which geopolitics played a huge role. This was not specific to Nepal. There is a growing body of literature that has shown tourism creating a distinctive national character of the destination. For example, Boissevan (1996) contends that tourism promotes self-awareness, pride, self-confidence, and solidarity among the host community by creating categories of 'we' and 'they'. Similarly, according to Wood (1993), while the packaging of tourist attractions has most often been analysed in terms of the images presented to foreigners and the way these images cater to foreign tourists' concerns with 'authenticity' and the like, it is evident that these images are increasingly bound up with local cultural politics as well, particularly as domestic tourism expands. In a pioneering work on Bali, Picard (1993) recognises tourism's far-reaching power to bring changes from within. He contends that the 'touristification' of Balinese culture should be considered within the context of the 'colonisation' of Bali and subsequent 'Indonesianisation' of Balinese culture, that is expected to foster both the development of tourism in Indonesia and the development of a national culture.

However, scholars have identified that the separation from the 'other' in tourism is more prominent in authoritarian states, where tourism is used to express the systemic political differences (Kim, Timothy and Han, 2007). Nepal in the 1960s was not very different. The development of modern tourism in Nepal started after the establishment of absolute monarchy in the 1960s. The new political system guided by absolute monarchy was justified by being built on Nepal's cultural uniqueness and claiming to 'embody indigenous characteristics of Nepal' (Poudyal, 1991). Tourism was used to advance the political project of forming a distinctive Nepali identity based on the hill culture and placed the Hindu monarchy at its core (Hachhethu, 2003). According to one participant,

> By conjoining Nepali identity with monarchy, Nepali nationalism was narrowly defined to the best interests of monarchy, because distancing oneself from the institution of Monarchy then became an anti-nationalist activity and treasonous. Within this framework, the touristic image of Shangri-La and exoticism became a very important tool to represent the monarch as a divine power to the perception of outside visitors and help advance a political process that was aimed at bolstering the King's position.

Since Kathmandu, the capital city, was rich in the cultural heritage of the Newari people, cultural tourism flourished in and around the Kathmandu valley. The presence of the monarch in most of the cultural festivals in the valley helped in two ways. First, in creating the 'Otherness' (Tnsescu, 2006) of Nepal, since the significance of touristic objects arises from what they are contrasted with: they represent something that is different from the everyday experience of the tourist (Urry, 2006), and secondly, it also helped boost the image of the king's power in Nepalese society and culture most prominently amongst visitors.

As far as institutionalisation was concerned, tourism was a royal project as it was started by a personal initiative from the royal family after the coronation of the then-king, in 1956, when the need for a tourism infrastructure was realised and gradually improved with the construction of hotels for accommodating dignitaries, guests, and journalists to this event (Chand, 2000; Piessel, 1990). The business of tourism largely remained under the control of the royal family and Kathmandu-based elites until 1990. The importance attached to tourism by the royal regime was such that the prince himself chaired a high-level committee that was constituted in 1972 with the task of drawing up a tourism master plan (Department of Tourism, 1972). The master plan outlined the need to develop Nepali distinctiveness by stressing a 'Nepal Style' of tourism. This was an indirect reference to the eminence of hill identity.

The royal interest in tourism extended from business to conservation efforts. The biggest travel agency and biggest hotel were owned by the royal family (*The Kathmandu Post* [TKP], 2006a). The biggest conservation trust, under a former king's name, looked after the conservation of natural resources and was managed directly by the then-prince. The trust managed one of the biggest conservation projects, popularly known as the Annapurna Area, which received about 115,000 foreign trekkers in 2016 to Nepal, almost four times more visitors than received by the famous Mt. Everest region in 2016 (MoTCA, 2016). The use of the Annapurna Area to advance the monarchy's interest is illustrated by Croes (2006) who argues that the monarchy used environmental conservation as a tool to renew and shore up its legitimacy during their direct rule (1960–1990). According to Croes, during the 1980s monarchical rule and its legitimacy were weakened by decades of development inertia and a series of palace scandals and rumours. The royal family dealt with the ecological crisis in the Himalayas in ways that were intended to address their crisis in legitimacy. The king visited the Annapurna region, Nepal's most popular trekking destination, and declared the need to protect the area's environment and later established it as a conservation project to help promote sustainable tourism – a measure that Croes (2006) argues was an attempt to renew a flagging monarchical legitimacy.

The government formed after the political change of 1990 strongly pursued capitalist policies, and there was a significant policy departure in the area of tourism. Tourism was given foremost priority in achieving the country's economic goals. However, there was a clear continuation of the centrality of monarchy in the national narrative of Nepal, and the touristic image of Nepal still relied on the Western-created image. It also advanced the agenda of constructing a singular Nepali 'national identity' and largely represented Nepal in a way that bolstered the invincibility of the institution of monarchy. For example, the idea of Shangri-La was indirectly encapsulated in the celebration of Visit Nepal 1998 that adopted the slogan 'A World of Its Own'. Similarly, the idea of 'mysticism' was intertwined with monarchy when launching a special tourism promotional programme that coined the slogan 'Mystical Kingdom-Destination Nepal' in 2002 and 2003. This was the time when the monarchy was in crisis because of the Maoists' insurgency and the negative image due to the Royal Palace massacre, in which the then-crown prince wiped out almost the entire royal family in 2001 (Bhandari, 2010). Similarly, the Himalayan mountains dominated the representation of tourism that was saturated with the images of the ethnic groups residing in those areas (Bott, 2009). For example, the Nepal Tourism Board (NTB) since its inception in 1999 promoted Nepal under the tagline: 'Mountains and more . . .', 'Mt Everest and more . . .', 'Naturally Nepal . . .' – all of them giving prominence to mountain imagery. A report claimed that tourism activities in Nepal are severely skewed in favour of a few areas, and the regional marketing of tourism is absent (Tourism for Rural Poverty Alleviation Programme, 2004).

Similarly, though royalty was not in any way a tourism product in itself, NTB used to prominently display photos of the reigning king and queen in every international travel and tourism fair and exhibition. Similarly, the NTB staff representing Nepal in all national and international fairs were strictly instructed to adhere to the dress code of the pre-1990 system. It required staff to be present in national dress, a continuation of the monocultural model of the political system of pre-1990. Even after the last royal regime was overthrown in 2006, a prominent issue erupted in that the NTB had supported the royal regime by publishing 5000 badges with pictures of the king and queen (TKP, 2006b), a controversy that led to the suspension of the then-CEO of the NTB.

In 2006, Nepal resolved its political conflict through an agreement between mainstream political parties and the Maoists, finally ending the decade-long armed insurgency. The previous pillars of national identity, the monarchy and the Hindu religion, were both abolished as the country was announced to be a secular republic. This has brought about a huge change in Nepal's national character, and the basis of Nepal's national identity has shifted from monarchy to republicanism, the people, and ethnic diversity. Much of this new narrative is the result of the agenda of the Communist parties over the last two decades. After the election to the Constitution Assembly in 2008, the Maoist Communist Party emerged as the largest party and was elected to government. As a result, national politics was dominated by the increasing influence of the leftist agenda and provided a stimulus for a policy change in tourism. A new Tourism Policy 2008 was introduced that acknowledged the policy context in the following ways: 'Subsequent to the ten years long people's war and historical popular movement . . . recognising the necessity of tourism promotion for economic change, the Government of Nepal has . . . declared to frame a new tourism policy . . .' (MoTCA, 2008).

The purpose of this policy was, partly, mobilising tourism for achieving social equity and community well-being; this is evidenced in the high priority given to small-scale community-led tourism activities as delivered through village tourism and homestay tourism. The policy states, '[T]his will develop ownership by the local community especially in the area of rural tourism and competitiveness in quality services' (MoTCA, 2008). A brand new Homestay Operations Directive (MoTCA, 2010) was formulated, 'in accordance with the objectives of increasing rural employment and lifestyle of rural underprivileged, women, Madheshi, ethnic minorities and other marginalised groups who have not been included in the development process enshrined in Tourism Policy the homestay intends to capture that essence'. According to a participant, such language of the directive correlates with the Maoist party's election manifesto that made the advancement of the underprivileged class or the 'proletariat' as its main goal. All of the above is confirmed by Scott (2010), who argues that tourism policy represents the aims and roles of the government. Scott argues that the aims of the policy can be associated with economic development, social equity and pro-poor tourism, employment, quality, visitor fulfilment, community well-being, cultural richness or environmental sustainability and many more.

Interestingly, the idea of homestay connects very well with the Maoist philosophy that advocates using people as a tool for revolution. Maoism views the industrial-rural divide as a major division exploited by capitalism, identifying capitalism as involving industrial urban developed 'First World' societies ruling over rural developing 'Third World' societies. It identifies peasant insurgencies in particular national contexts as part of a context of world revolution, in which the global countryside would overwhelm the global cities. For Maoists, villages and rural areas are the focus of their strategy, and the idea of homestay in the rural community connects strongly with their own idea of revolution. This could be the reason that there were no deliberations on the potential threat that homestay can bring to local culture or peoples' way of life, despite there being so many examples that have shown the impacts of tourism on host communities and their implications (Buzinde and Santos, 2009; Jackson and Inbakaran, 2006; Lepp, 2008; Ryan and Cave, 2005). Since the above political change, there has been more demand for the diversification of tourism activities across the regions. With the provincial governments in office now, the cultural stereotypes created in earlier periods of tourism development in Nepal are challenged, and there is a gradual change in tourism representation. For example, the Nepal Tourism Board has begun to appreciate local initiatives and is now more supportive of them. For example, it has intensified the need for organising more tourism activities targeted at domestic visitors in various parts of the country. A participant associated with the Board said,

> There is a changed political context in Nepal. The new Constitution has restructured Nepal into a federal republic. We have to accommodate ourselves to this new set up and make sure our priorities and activities are commensurate with the ideas of inclusion of Nepal's varied diversity in its development efforts. Thus, we are working towards projecting this new image of Nepal.

Another participant working in a public-sector tourism institution said, 'with the growing debate of federalism, the term inclusiveness and ethnic identity has become very popular and we need to see how we can address this through tourism'. A respondent from the tourism industry in a western region of Nepal stated,

> I believe that with the new set of federal state governments the situation has started to change. All the provincial governments have identified tourism as one of the growth sectors. There is a competition amongst these provincial governments in bringing more tourists and tourism investments in their provinces. Since these provinces themselves are newly formed, it might take time for them, but they will definitely need a branding exercise for pitching their tourism distinctiveness. This will compel the NTB to change the way it has been projecting Nepal in international forums.

The acceptance of tourism's need to diversify its base in order to address the question of exclusion of provincial identity means that the future of tourism may start to focus on products other than traditional ones. The increased pressure for the diversification of tourism may also be attributed, to some extent, to the transitional period of political fluidity, but what seems certain is that tourism's traditional geographical and sociocultural domain will definitely be contested by the new areas and ethnic groups, bringing a fresh challenge to the managers of tourism in the country. This is in conjunction with the changed narrative of national identity created by the new Constitution.

Conclusion

This chapter has discussed the trajectory of Nepali nationalism in the recent past and shown how tourism has followed this line to project the 'national' account. I have suggested that the image of Nepal was partly created by the Western imagination, which fitted perfectly with the interests of the regime, and so tourism representations were deliberately selected to exploit the 'nationalist' intent of the regime. In fact, this narrative of Nepal continued even after the fall of absolute monarchy in the 1990, and tourism agencies pursued the same narrative in Nepal's representation in tourism, notwithstanding the need to present the 'real' Nepal in the changed context. The chapter also appreciates that the foundation of the new national identity laid by the new constitution has warranted a change in narrative, and there is a need for wider debate on what should be the symbol of Nepal's tourism in the changed context.

I have also argued in this chapter that monarchy had an influential role in the development of tourism, which was driven by the political interests of strengthening their legitimacy. As such, tourism was grounded in Nepal's image of Shangri-La or the exotic kingdom, which put monarchy at the centre of Nepal's national imagery. This image was so strong that even after the abolition of monarchy, tourism continued to rely on this identity, and there is a gap in the representation of Nepal and the existing imagery of Nepal, which is strongly tilted towards the Himalayan heritage, and the regions that fall outside such imagery are largely absent in the nation's tourism iconography. A good example of such unbalanced tourism representations can be taken from the Terai. There is very little awareness of tourism activity in the Terai region, though some prominent tourism activities are based in this area. Nepal's wildlife tourism is primarily concentrated in the wildlife conservation areas located in Terai. For example, the Chitwan National Park is the most-often-visited national park – receiving three times more visitors than the famous Mt. Everest region. A similar case is that of Janakpurdham, another important Hindu pilgrimage shrine in the region. Interestingly, the core of Nepal's cultural tourism, which relies on Buddhist heritage, originates from the famous Lumbini, birthplace of Lord Buddha, which is in Terai. In the next chapter, I will argue that the issue of exclusion of this region in Nepal tourism representation is the continuation of a particular version of nationalism.

References

Anderson, B. (1991). *Imagined Communities: Reflections on the Origin and Spread of Nationalism*. London: Verso.

Ashworth, G. J. (1994). From History to Heritage-from Heritage to Identity: In Search of Concepts and Models. In G. L. Ashworth and P. J. Larkham (Eds.), *Building a New Heritage: Tourism, Culture and Identity* (pp. 13–30). London: Routledge.

Ashworth, G. J. (1998). Tourism in the Communication of Senses of Place or Displacement in New Mexico. *Tourism Culture and Communication*, 1(1), 97–107.

Barth, F. (1981). Ethnic Groups and Boundaries. In *Process and Form in Social Life: Selected Essays of Fredrik Barth: Volume* (pp. 198–227). London: Routledge and Kegan Paul.

Bhabha, H. (1992). Postcolonial Criticism. In S. Greenblatt and G. Gunn (Eds.), *Redrawing the Boundaries* (pp. 437–465). New York: The Modern Language Association of America.

Bhandari, K. (2010). Tourism in Nepal: Post-Monarchy Challenges. *Journal of Tourism and Cultural Change*, 8(1), 69–83.

Bhattachan, K. B. (2009). Discourse on Social Exclusion and Inclusion in Nepal: Old Wine in a New Bottle. In *Identity and Society: Social Exclusion and Inclusion in Nepal* (pp. 11–43). Kathmandu: Social Inclusion Research Fund.

Blaikie, P., Cameron, J. and Seddon, D. (1980). *Nepal in Crisis: Growth and Stagnation at the Periphery*. Oxford: Clarendon Press.

Boissevan, J. (1996). *Coping with Tourists: European Relations to Mass Tourism*. Oxford: Berghann Books.

Bott, E. (2009). Big Mountain, Big Name: Globalised Relations of Risk in Himalayan Mountaineering. *Journal of Tourism and Cultural Change*, 7(4), 287–301.

Breuilly, J. (2013). *The Oxford Handbook of the History of Nationalism*. Oxford: Oxford University Press.

Brubaker, W. R. (1992). *Citizenship and Nationhood in France and Germany*. Cambridge, MA: Harvard University Press.

Burghart, R. (1984). The Formation of the Concept of Nation-State in Nepal. *Journal of Asian Studies*, 44(1), 101–125.

Buzinde, C. N. and Santos, C. A. (2009). Interpreting Slavery Tourism. *Annals of Tourism Research*, 36, 439–458.

Chalmers, R. (2003). 'We Nepalis': Language, Literature and the Formation of Nepali Public Sphere in India, 1914–1940. *Unpublished Ph.D. dissertation*, School of Oriental and African Studies, University of London.

Chand, D. (2000). *Nepal's Tourism Uncensored Facts*, Varanasi: Pilgrims Publishing.

Conversi, D. (1995). Reassessing Current Theories of Nationalism: Nationalism as Boundary Maintenance and Creation. *Nationalism and Ethnic Politics*, 1(1), 73–85.

Croes, K. D. (2006). Conserving the King: Inverting the Origin Story of the Annapurna Conservation Area Project of Nepal. *Himalaya, the Journal of the Association for Nepal and Himalayan Studies*, 26(1), 11–18.

Datta-Ray, S. K. (2013). *Smash and Grab: Annexation of Sikkim*. New Delhi: Westland.

Department of Tourism. (1972). *Tourism Master Plan 1972*. Kathmandu: His Majesty's Government of Nepal.

Dirlik, A. (1996). Chinese History and the Question of Orientalism. *History and Theory*, 35(4), 96–118.

Gaige, F. H. (1975). *Regionalism and National Unity in Nepal*. New Delhi: Vikas Publishing House.

Geertz, C. (1973). *Interpretation of Cultures: Selected Essays*. London: Fontana.

Gellner, D. (2001). How Should One Study Ethnicity and Nationalism. *Contributions to Nepalese Studies*, 28(1), 1–10.

Gellner, D., Pfaff-Czarnecka, J. P. and Whelpton, J. (2008). *Nationalism and Ethnicity in Nepal*. Kathmandu: Vajra Publications.

Gellner, E. (1964). *Thought and Change*. London: Weidenfield and Nicolson.

Gellner, E. (1983). *Nations and Nationalism*. Ithaca, NY: Cornell University Press.

Giri, R. A. (2010). Cultural Anarchism: The Consequences of Privileging Languages in Nepal. *Journal of Multilingual and Multicultural Development*, 31(10), 87–100.

Greenfeld, L. (1995). Nationalism in Western and Eastern Europe Compared. In S. E. Hanson and W. Spohn (Eds.), *Can Europe Work? Germany & the Reconstruction of Postcommunist Societies* (pp. 15–23). Seattle: University of Washington Press.

Gurung, O., Tamang, M. S. and Turin, M. (2014). *Perspectives on Social Inclusion and Exclusion in Nepal*. Kathmandu: Tribhuwan University Central Department of Sociology/Anthropology.

Hachhethu, K. (2003). Democracy and Nationalism: Interface between State and the Ethnicity in Nepal. *Contributions to Nepalese Studies*, 30(2), 217–252.

Hamilton, F. B. (1819). *An Account of the Kingdom of Nepal*. Edinburgh: Archibald Constable.

Hobsbawm, E. (1983). Introduction: Inventing Traditions. In E. Hobsbawm and T. Ranger (Eds.), *The Invention of Tradition* (pp. 1–14). Cambridge: Cambridge University Press.

Hobsbawm, E. (1999). *Nations and Nationalism since 1780*. Cambridge: Cambridge University Press.

Hobsbawm, E. and Ranger, T. (1983). *The Invention of Tradition*. Cambridge: Cambridge University Press.

Hutchinson, J. (1999). Re-Interpreting Cultural Nationalism. *Australian Journal of Politics and History*, 45(3), 392–407.

Hutchinson, J. (2001). Nations and Culture. In M. Guibernau and J. Hutchison (Eds.), *Understanding Nationalism* (pp. 74–96). Cambridge: Polity Press.

Hutt, M. (1996). Looking for Shangri-La, from Hilton to Lamicchane. In T. Selwyn (Ed.), *The Tourist Image: Myths and Myth-Making in Tourism* (pp. 49–60). Chichester: John Wiley & Sons.

Hutt, M. (2012). Singing New Nepal. *Nations and Nationalism*, 18(2), 306–325.

Jackson, J. and Molokotos-Leiderman, L. (2014). *Nationalism, Ethnicity and Boundaries: Conceptualising and Understanding Identity through Boundary Approaches*. London: Routledge.

Jackson, M. S. and Inbakaran, R. J. (2006). Evaluating Residents' Attitudes and Intentions to Act towards Tourism Development in Regional Victoria, Australia. *International Journal of Tourism Research*, 8(5), 355–366.

Jenkins, R. (1995). Nations and Nationalism: Towards More Open Models. *Nations and Nationalism*, 1(3), 369–390.

The Kathmandu Post (TKP). (2006a). King Has Shares in 17 Companies, August 27. Available at: www.kantipuronline.com/kolnews.php?&nid=84179 (accessed 8 September 2009).

The Kathmandu Post (TKP). (2006b). NTB Misused Funds to Please Royal Regime, June 23. Available at: www.kantipuronline.com/kolnews.php?&nid=77574 (accessed 8 September 2009).

Kazi, J. N. (1993). *Inside Sikkim: Against the Tide*. Gangtok: Hill Media Publications.

Kim, S. S., Timothy, D. J. and Han, H. (2007). Tourism and Political Ideologies: A Case of Tourism in North Korea. *Tourism Management*, 28(4), 1031–1043.

Lawoti, M. (2005). *Towards Democratic Nepal: Inclusive Political Institutions for Multicultural Society*. New Delhi: Sage Publications.

Lawoti, M. and Hangen, S. (2013). *Nationalism and Ethnic Conflict in Nepal*. London: Routledge.

Lecomte-Tilouine, M. (2009). *Hindu Kingship, Ethnic Revival, and Maoist Rebellion in Nepal*. New Delhi: Oxford University Press.

Lepp, A. (2008). Attitudes towards Initial Tourism Development in a Community with No Prior Tourism Experience: The Case of Bigodi, Uganda. *Journal of Sustainable Tourism*, 16, 5–22.

Liechty, M. (2017). *Far Out: Countercultural Seekers and the Tourist Encounter in Nepal*. Chicago: University of Chicago Press.

Maguire, S. (2016). Brother Jonathan and John Bell a Nation: The transactional nature of American Nationalism in the early Nineteenth century. *National Identities*, 18(2), 179–198.

Malagodi, M. (2008). Forging the Nepali Nation through Law: A Reflection on the Use of Western Legal Tools in a Himalayan Kingdom. *Studies in Ethnicity and Nationalism*, 8(3), 433–452.

Malagodi, M. (2013). *Constitutional Nationalism and Legal Exclusion: Equality, Identity Politics and Democracy in Nepal (1990–2007)*. New Delhi: Oxford University Press.

McCrone, D. and McPherson, G. (2009). *National Days: Constructing and Mobilising National Identity*. Basingstoke: Palgrave Macmillan.

Ministry of Culture, Tourism and Civil Aviation (MoTCA). (2016). *Nepal Tourism Statistics (2016)*. Kathmandu: Government of Nepal.

Ministry of Tourism and Civil Aviation (MoTCA). (2008). *Paryatan Niti*. Available at: www.tourismdepartment.gov.np/acts-regulations.

Ministry of Tourism and Civil Aviation (MoTCA). (2010). *Homestay Karyabidhi*. Available at: www.tourism.gov.np/pdf/Homstay-karyabidhi2067-3-27.pdf.

Nairn, T. (1981). *The Break-Up of Britain Crisis and Neo-Nationalism*. London: Verso.

Ong, A. (1998). *Flexible Citizenship: The Cultural Logics of Transnationality*. Durham, NC: Duke University Press.

Onta, P. (1996). Creating a Brave Nepali Nation in British India: The Rhetoric of Jati Improvement, Rediscovery of Bhanubhakta and the Writing of Bir History. *Studies in Nepali History and Society*, 1(1), 37–76.

Picard, M. (1993). Cultural Tourism in Bali: National Integration and Regional Differentiation. In M. Hitchcock, V. T. King and M. J. G. Parnwall (Eds.), *Tourism in Southeast Asia* (pp. 71–98). London: Routledge.

Piessel, M. (1990). *Tiger for Breakfast*. New Delhi: Time Books International.

Poudyal, A. R. (1991). Nation, Nationalism and Some Issues of National Consensus. *Contributions to Nepalese Studies*, 18(1), 41–51.

Pradhan, K. (1982). *Pahilo Pahar*. Darjeeling: Shyam Prakashan.

Quigley, D. (1987). Ethnicity without Nationalism: The Newars of Nepal. *European Journal of Sociology*, 28(1), 152–170.

Rademacher, A. (2007). Farewell to the Bagmati Civilisation: Losing Riverscape and Nation in Kathmandu. *National Identities*, 9(2), 127–142.

Rose, G. (1995). Place and Identity: A Sense of Place. In D. Massey and P. Jess (Eds.), *A Place in the World? Places, Culture and Globalisation* (pp. 87–132). New York: Oxford University Press.

Rose, L. E. (1971). *Nepal: Strategy for Survival*. Berkeley, CA: University of California Press.

Ryan, C. and Cave, J. (2005). Structuring Destination Image: A Qualitative Approach. *Journal of Travel Research*, 44(2), 143–150.

Sahlins, P. (1989). *Boundaries: The Making of France and Spain in the Pyrenees*. Berkeley, CA: University of California Press.

Said, E. (1991). *Orientalism*. London: Penguin.

Scott, N. (2010). *Tourism Policy: A Strategic Review: Contemporary Tourism Reviews*. Oxford: Goodfellow Publishers. Available at: www.goodfellow publishers.com/free_files/fileTourismPolicy.pdf.

Shah, G. (2012). *Mulukai Narahe Hami Kasari Nepali?* Available at: http://onlinekhabar.com/2012/03/134726.html (accessed 16 March 2012).

Sharma, P. (2012). Some Aspects of Nepal's Social Demography: Update 2011. *Studies in Nepali History and Society*, 17(2), December.

Shils, E. (1957). Primordial, Personal, Sacred and Civil Ties. *British Journal of Sociology*, 7, 113–145.

Shneiderman, S. (2014). Reframing Ethnicity: Academic Tropes, Recognition Beyond Politics, and Ritualized Action between Nepal and India. *American Anthropologist*, 116(2), 279–295.

Smith, A. D. (1986). *The Ethnic Origins of Nation*. New York: Blackwell Publishing.

Smith, A. D. (1991). *National Identity*. London: Penguin.

Smith, A. D. (2000). Theories of Nationalism: Alternative Models of Nation Formation. In M. Leifer (Ed.), *Asian Nationalism* (pp. 1–20). London: Routledge.

Smith, A. D. (2008). *The Cultural Foundations of Nations*. Hoboken, NJ: Blackwell Publishing.

Smith, A. D. (2009). *Ethno-Symbolism and Nationalism: A Cultural Approach*. New York: Routledge.

Stephens, A. C. (2013). *The Persistence of Nationalism: From Imagined Communities to Urban Encounters*. New York: Routledge.

Subba, T. B. (2002). Nepal and the Indian Nepalis. In K. M. Dixit and S. Ramachandran (Eds.), *State of Nepal* (pp. 119–136). Kathmandu: Himal Books.

Tilly, C. (2005). *Ties That Bind . . . and Bound Identities, Boundaries, and Social Ties*. Boulder, CO: Paradigm Press.

Tnsescu, A. (2006). Tourism, Nationalism and Post-Communist Romania: The Life and Death of Dracula Park. *Journal of Tourism and Cultural Change*, 4(3), 159–176.

Tourism for Rural Poverty Alleviation Programme. (2004). *Tourism Marketing Strategy for Nepal 2005–2020*. Kathmandu: TRPAP.

Urry, J. (2006). *The Tourist Gaze*. London: Sage Publications.

Van den Berghe, Pierre L. (1995). Does Race Matter? *Nations and Nationalism*, 1(3), 357–368.

Wimmer, A. (2013). *Ethnic Boundary Making: Institutions, Power, Networks*. Oxford Studies in Culture and Politics. New York: Oxford University Press.

Wood, R. E. (1993). Tourism, Culture and Sociology of Development. In M. Hitchcock, V. T. King and M. J. G. Parnwell (Eds.), *Tourism in South-East Asia* (pp. 48–70). London: Routledge.

Yan, G. and Santos, S. A. (2009). China, Forever: Tourism Discourse and Self-Orientalism. *Annals of Tourism Research*, 36(2), 296–315.

Zhang, X. (2006). The Globalized Logic of Orientalism. *Contemporary Chinese Thought*, 37(4), 48–54.

3 'National' imagery in tourism representations

This chapter looks into the representations of Nepali national character in the activities of a tourism agency, using three examples from tourism representations: a museum, a promotional CD-ROM, and the design of the Visit Nepal 2020 logo. It examines the range of icons and images, symbols in the above examples, and the accompanying narrative of the Nepali nation. I have noted in the previous chapter that the version of Nepali national identity advanced by the monarchical regime associated 'Nepaliness' with Himalayan heritage and hill culture and fails to acknowledge the multiplicity of vernacular identities. This chapter shows that the imagery of Nepal in the various tourism mediums above continues to express that version of Nepali national identity. It also identifies that it would be helpful if tourism representation attempts to appreciate countries' regional aspirations and diversity.

Symbols, uniforms, ceremonies, and monuments are important ways through which visitors are reminded of the heritage and culture of a destination. It is also an important way in which the nation is narrated to its members. French sociologist Lanfant acknowledges the role of heritage tourism in shaping identity and depicting 'nationness' through such narration. She writes, 'imperceptibly the place becomes determined by external forces and reconstructed from a touristic point of view' (1995, p. 5). The system of the promotion of tourism indirectly intervenes in cultural references, in the definition of the values, signs, supports, and markers of identity (1995, p. 8), and can greatly define and dictate the positioning of identity and foster a sense of distinctiveness.

Scholars take the view that host societies choose tourism sites to represent something about their society to the world (Chambers, 2000), and this is often grounded in relations of power (Morgan and Pritchard, 1998; see also Ateljvic and Doorne, 2002; Light, 2001), in which discourse plays a huge part. This chapter is based on the idea that the discourse produced by tourism through various touristic outlets, attractions, and representations can have greater repercussions in creating an identity. Hall (1996) considers that representations are important in constituting identity because

> Identities are about questions of using the resources of history, language and culture in the process of becoming rather than being: not 'who we are' or 'where we come from'; so much as what we might become, how we have been represented and how that bears on how we might represent ourselves. Identities are therefore constituted within, not outside representation.

(p. 4)

Scholars describe representation as a real account (Brown, 1995, p. 135) and consider it a means to convey the discourses of destination image (Ryan, 2002). Representations can also be described as the 'order of appearance of a thing or event, according to conventions' (Hollinshead, 2000, p. 501). They are very important in conveying the meaning of an activity that would otherwise take a very long time to convey. According to Geertz (1995, p. 43), without them it is highly unlikely that anyone could grasp 'so vast a thing as an entire way of life and (find) the words to describe it'. However, representations do not exist independently; they exist within the context of one's own social reality, inherited from the past in the form of narratives and accounts found in books, travel autobiographies, and newspapers about other places (Hunter, 2008). Thus, the study of touristic representations in this chapter helps us understand how the narrative of Nepali identity is constructed and why and how these representations have dominated the narrative of Nepali identity.

MacCannell (1999), who calls tourism more than 'merely a collection of random material representations', identifies the immense role of tourism in the creation of image and perception about a place or its people. He claims, 'when they appear in itineraries, they have a moral claim on the tourists and, at the same time, they tend toward universality, incorporating natural, social, historical and cultural domains in a single representation made possible by the tour' (1999, p. 45). Other scholars have argued that promotional images in tourism are the reflection of the prevailing cultural values of a society, and they play an important role in shaping these values and contributing to the process of socialisation (Morgan and Pritchard, 1998). This implies that the narrative of a nation recounted in touristic discourses should not be taken simply as a consumptive issue related to branding. It is also the way through which, with or without its awareness, a nation can frame its society and culture and express its nationhood and national identity.

My emphasis on representation is grounded on McCrone, Morris, and Kiely's (1995, p. 207) argument that the assertion of identity itself is the main ingredient of identity: thus, the representation of Nepal made in tourism discourse, irrespective of its appropriateness, is meaningful in understanding the nature of 'national' consciousness. Butler (1998) suggests a similar conclusion. Discussing the case of Scottish tourism imagery, he suggests that whether or not tartanry or images of the Scottish Highlands that tourism appropriated were true representations of Scotland, it created a great cultural distinction and still assumes enormous relevance as a potent signifier of Scottishness to most visitors (Butler, 1998). Amidst such a backdrop, it is important to see how tourism aids the 'national' sense by narrating the story of Nepali nationhood through the representation of national icons, emblems, and symbols.

However, discussion of the role of symbols in the formation or articulation of national unity has received very limited coverage in scholarship, with the exception of Billig (1995) and Smith (2009). Smith (1999), in his theory of 'ethno-symbolism', treats the symbols of the nation as part of the ethno-cultural heritage which modern nationalists can make use of to forge a national unity and identity (cf. Kolsto, 2006). He considers that together with symbols, the myths, values, and memories of the group fulfil the same function. Analysing nationalism in more established states, Billig (1995) argues that national flags play a huge role in these states on a symbolic level. Billig claims that the difference between established and unestablished states is the one between 'the flag hanging unnoticed on the public building' and 'a flag which is being consciously waved with fervent passion' (Billig, 1995, p. 8). However, what is unexplored is how the use of a national flag in the touristic medium evokes a sense of nationhood and nationality.

I will now examine the tourism representations through three mediums: (a) an ethnographic museum, (b) a promotional CD-ROM, and (c) the design of the Visit Nepal Year 2020 logo. I will focus on the issue of diversity in these mediums with particular focus on the Terai or Madhesh. Terai or *Madhesh* is used interchangeably to refer to Nepal's southern plains. Though the term 'Terai' was commonly used until 2006, increased regional politics has almost displaced it by another term '*Madhesh*' which bears a more political connotation. The idea of Madhesh and Madheshi identity is strongly liked to nationalism. This is because nationalism in Nepal meant maintaining its distinctiveness compared to India (Grandin, 1996). This 'nationalist' mindset sees the entire Terai as more akin to India because of the Madhesis' cultural proximity to India (Gaige, 1975). According to Grandin, the imagery from the Terai region would look suspiciously Indian in the eyes of the Nepalese, while pictures of mountainous Nepal are well suited to assert the distinction from India.

As a challenge to this perception, the use of '*Madhesh*' itself was a defiance against the state and the 'alleged' exclusion and discrimination against the people of this region. The political parties and groups who are fighting for the rights of the *Madhesi* people fervently avoid using the term 'Terai'. However, there is also a greater debate on what constitutes *Madhesh*, and scholars argue that not all parts of the Terai can be considered *Madhesh*. For example, Chitwan, which partly is in the southern plains, has always been regarded as inner Terai and is distinctively different from *Madhesh* in terms of demography, culture, and habitation. This perception has a significant effect on the development of tourism in Terai, as Hepburn (2002) notices that Indians are not considered tourists in Nepal. The cultural heritage of Terai is akin to north Indian heritage and would be of interest to Indian tourists, who are the largest market. According to MoTCA (2016), about 120,000 Indians visited Nepal by air in 2016, and visitors by land remain uncounted due to the open border between Nepal and India.

The region of Terai was particularly chosen because this region occupies an important role in Nepal. Terai comprises 17 percent of the total geographical area. Almost half of Nepal's total population resides here. The indigenous people of Terai are called the *Madhesi*. The three major ethnic groups of the region – the Maithili-, Awadi-, and Bhojpuri-speaking peoples comprise 19.6 percent of Nepal's total population (Sharma, 2012). Though there is a larger debate on what constitutes the Terai region and who are *Madhesi*, three predominant ethnic groups speaking Maithili, Awadi, and Bhojpuri have been referred to as the *Madhesi* in this paper. Though confined within a very limited area, tourism in this region cannot be ignored altogether. Two prominent tourism destinations in the region are Lumbini and Chitwan. Lumbini alone received 1.2 million tourists in 2016, including Nepali nationals. Chitwan received 88,000 foreign tourists in 2016, which far exceeds the total number of tourists received by the famous Annapurna region (MoTCA, 2016). Additionally, more than 150,000 third-country tourists enter Nepal through various entry points of Terai, which makes this region a major tourist transit point from India. The representation of Terai means the presentation of the natural and cultural heritage of that region, which could include landscape, flora and fauna, people, and culture.

A museum, a promotional CD-ROM, and a tourism promotional logo were chosen for this study because they are three completely different tourism products, and diverse objects of study in research help to validate research findings, increase its reliability and assist the generalisation of its results. Additionally, museums are institutions closely intertwined with the collective memory of nations (Zolberg, 1996) and national identity. McLean (2005) is of the view that through the authority vested in them, museums authenticate and present identities through the presentation of heritage. Another object chosen for this study, the promotional CD-ROM, is a popular information-dissemination tool and one of the most potent mediums through which a national story is told to prospective visitors. The narration presented in the CD-ROM gives an impression of the characteristics of the nation, and it plays a role in bolstering national image.

The reason for choosing the Visit Nepal 2020 logo was informed by the argument that the use of national signifiers in commercial enterprises and promotion has the element of the creation of a boundary. Some scholars have associated such endeavours as an example of commercial nationalism, which is described as 'a continuation and extension of the overall theme, style and symbol of the official nationalism' (White, 2017, p. 8). In a practical sense, official and commercial nationalisms are very much the same in their messages, though they may be different in the way they present their visual or textual representations (Ratz and Irimias, 2017). Despite being a commercial venture, the design of a logo by state agencies cannot go too far away from the stances of official nationalism and on many occasions utilises the symbols of official nationalism such as national symbols, flags, images, and icons. The discussion around the Visit Nepal Year 2020 logo sheds light on such a form of creating a distinctive national identity.

The ethnographic museum at NTB

An important place where the semiotics of nation can be presented is at museums. Museums are often seen as places to produce national discourse. They can be the venue to present a desired ideology, because as an important component of heritage they are repositories of identity. McLean (2005) is of the view that through the authority vested in them, museums authenticate and present identities through the presentation of heritage. Pitchford (2008) has shown how museums and other attractions that focus on a group's history and culture serve as a medium to project ethnic and nationalist messages and help to build a revalued collective identity. Museums are a major resource and a ubiquitous tourist attraction in many countries. According to Anderson, assertion of a common sense of identity is important in national imagining, to which museums, sacred sites, and monuments are a medium to create an image of and to spread the sense of community. Pitchford (2006) has shown that tourists who visit Wales are exposed to almost every piece of the national story in some form: museums and other attractions that focus on a group's history and culture serve as a medium to project ethnic and nationalist messages and help to build a revalued collective identity.

The Nepal National Ethnographic Museum is located in the NTB office premises. The museum is housed in the two halls of the NTB and is managed under the joint aegis of the tourist board and a non-governmental organisation, the Nepal National Ethnographic Museum (NNEM). The NNEM was constituted with the original aim of opening a larger open-air ethnographic museum. Since realising its long-term goal of establishing an open-air museum needed more time and resources, the NNEM board came up with the idea of setting up a museum in the two halls of NTB with the artefacts it had collected for the larger museum project. The NTB provided the full financial resources to construct the dioramas and organise the collection. The NNEM in association with the NTB contacted different ethnic groups and organisations and requested them to volunteer in collecting ethnic artefacts and organising their display. Each ethnic group was allocated one diorama. The museum was inaugurated in 2003 by the then-crown prince, and for this reason it displayed the portraits of the crown prince and princess at the information counter until the monarchy was abolished. The museum charges entrance fees to its visitors. The NTB oversees the task of marketing and the promotion of the museum and has produced brochures, posters, and a webpage. The NTB official informed that it offers a museum tour on the itinerary of all of its international invitees who visit Nepal on familiarisation tours. The museum claims that it provides a kaleidoscopic image of Nepal to visitors (NTBa, undated).

The museum displays permanent exhibitions of 12 ethnic groups of Nepal, namely: *Thakali, Sherpa, Tamang, Gurung, Rai, Limbu, Chepang, Jyapu* of the Newar group, *Magar, Sunwar, Tharu,* and *Brahmins.* Its exhibits are dominated by hill tribes or groups from the mountainous region. There is only one ethnic group the *Tharu* who originally hail from northern Terai or inner Terai. Any other ethnic group from Terai is conspicuously absent. This exclusion is contradictory to the objective of the museum, which hopes that the museum helps promote public interest in Nepal's rich cultural makeup and contributes to the process of national integration and national pride (NTBa, undated).

When I tried to find the reason for the exclusion of Terai-based ethnicities or the *Madhesi*, most of the respondents had never realised that the *Madhesi* deserve a place in the museum, because for them *Madhesi* do not fall in the common imagination of Nepalis for tourists. For example, a participant stated,

Tourism identity of Nepal is all about Himalayas and the people and culture that live in and around high mountains. It is full of references to trekking and mountaineering, mountain peaks, mountain communities. As such, representation of those who are beyond the above identity is not necessary for a museum that is primarily opened for educating the tourists about Nepal.

The above view is important because, according to this participant, museums are solely intended for foreign tourists. Such an idea also fails to comprehend that touristic representations are as important to Nepalis as for foreign tourists, as studies have shown that representations in museums are an important medium to instil a sense of inclusion and belongingness to a national community. However, there was an alternative explanation that this exclusion was more related to logistic problems. According to the NTB official looking after the museum, when the museum was being set-up no credible Madhesi group came up with an interest to have themselves represented in it. He stated that

> The Museum was a collective effort because after we decided about it, we contacted various ethnic groups requesting them to send us their artefacts that could be included in the Museum. None of the *Madheshi* groups came forward with their artefacts or exhibits and no one requested that they needed to be included. So we only decided to go with those who had already sent us their collections or those who provided commitment that they would do so.

However, the above view was contradicted by another participant. The absence of *Madhesi* was deliberate to an extent, said another participant. His view was,

> the dominant perception of Nepal for tourists is based on the image of Himalayan Shangri-la; the presence of *Madhesi* would be a mismatch to this image . . . That is why we were not keen on getting them onboard in the Museum project.

The case of hill *Brahmin* is different, though. According to one participant, when the museum finally took shape, a senior NTB executive who looked after the museum project took extra initiatives to have *Brahmins* represented in the museum. But by the time they were to be inducted, all the allocated dioramas had run out, and the only space available was inside a dome-shaped Buddhist Stupa originally designed for the information counter. Being in the highest pyramid of the Hindu caste system, the *Brahmins* refused to be housed in the Buddhist dome and instead demanded an open space. In the end, they were provided a small space outside the built-in diorama. This is why all ethnic groups except the *Brahmins* are housed in the dioramas, said a museum official. A participant opined that not all groups can be represented in a small museum like this and that when the larger project of an open-air museum is realised everyone can be properly accommodated, making reference to the ambitious plan of an open-air ethnographic museum in future.

An important departure is seen in this ethnographic museum when compared with similar initiatives elsewhere. Ethnographic museums originated specifically in the search to preserve the 'exotic', 'preliterate', 'primitive', 'simple', 'savage', or 'vanishing races' (Morgan and Pritchard, 1998). But it is interesting that the NTB and the museum staff deemed it necessary to include 'privileged' *Brahmins* while not reaching out to any 'more qualifying' ethnic group from the Terai region. There is an opinion that the fluidity of national identity in an era of multiculturalism makes the task of museums challenging (McLean, 2005). This is because unlike in the past, museums today, while narrating the nation, have the task of narrating its diversity. The case of the Ethnographic Museum shows us that it has failed to appreciate the multiplicity of heritage in Nepal.

There has been a study elsewhere which has shown that the unity of a nation cannot be compromised but is strengthened by acknowledging its diversity. For example, the study of the National Museum of Scotland shows that it is constructing multifarious readings that reflect both their individual identities and their collective identities (McLean and Cooke, 2003). They also find that in addition to the traditional 'mythic' identity of Scotland, museum visitors make contemporary readings of the identities which are shaped by the contemporary political and cultural understanding of the nation of Scotland. This is evidence that appreciating individual identities enhances collective identity, and the inclusion of *Madhesi* does not undermine but strengthens Nepali national identity.

The promotional CD-ROM

In the theory of tourism, visuality forms a core element. According to Urry (2006), tourists look into a set of different scenes, landscapes, or townscapes with great interest and curiosity. He argues that tourists 'gaze' at what they encounter, and this gaze varies by society, by social group, and by historical period. According to him, these visual images are cultural products that create distinctive sociocultural effects in close relation to social conditions of viewing and reading. Tourism, having an experiential nature, relies more on visual practices to promote and represent destinations. This has increased the role of digital media in recent years because it can now provide high-quality visual experience of the place through its interactive interface and virtual-reality technologies. Butler (1990) proposes that visual media are particularly convincing and effective in shaping images and increasing visitation. It has become important because such media can provide an enormous capacity to portray the destination's culture, people, and identity in a compelling manner.

The CD-ROM is one of the most preferred means for tourism promotion by NTB. They are distributed free of charge at international tourism fairs and road shows. Nepalis going abroad are provided with free copies so that they can disseminate them through their own channels. The CD-ROM informs viewers of all the special features of Nepal as a tourist destination and gives information on the country, people, and culture, tourism destinations within the country, and the activities offered (NTBb, undated). In the entire CD-ROM there is no mention of the term 'Madhesh'. It uses 'Terai' to refer to this region, probably in a bid to distance itself from any political misinterpretation. In the first section of the CD-ROM that introduces the country, its people and ethnic mosaic mentions the major ethnic groups except the Madhesi. It refers to Sherpas, Gurungs, Thakali, Tamangs, Rais and Limbus, Tharus, Chetris and Thakuris, Brahmans, Newars, Chepangs and Kusundas, Magars, Managis, Dolpa – all hill tribes except the Tharus.

The CD-ROM makes extensive use of pictorial photographs to showcase Nepal's myriad tourism features. It has a photo gallery with a collection of 50 photographs of landscape and cultural heritage of the country. These are divided into five sub-categories: adventure, flora and fauna, landscape, monuments, and people and culture – each having 10 photographs. There is no photograph of Terai-based activities in the adventure section despite the fact that wildlife adventures are based in this region. The sub-category of flora and fauna represents exclusively hill and mountain natural heritage. The landscape section is full of photographs of hill landscapes with snow-capped mountains in the background. In the monuments section, 9 out of 10 pictures are from the Kathmandu valley, and the remaining one is from Terai. Even Lumbini is conspicuously absent. Seven of those monuments are Hindu shrines: the remaining three are a Buddhist temple, a clock tower, and the Central Secretariat building of the government of Nepal. In the section on people and culture, two photographs are of Terai: one of a Hindu religious festival and other of an ethnic Terai house; six are of Kathmandu-based shrines and two from other mountain peoples.

There are 30 assorted videos of varying but short length in the CD-ROM. Two videos are from the Terai region, one a Hindu shrine and another a Buddhist temple. Both of them have no commentary. Videos that feature outdoor activities have no Terai-based footage. A video on World Heritage Sites has the commentary, 'The Kathmandu Valley alone has seven of the world's most important heritage sites'. What follows then is footage of heritage sites of the Kathmandu Valley. There is neither any mention of Lumbini nor any Lumbini footage. Lumbini is listed in the UNESCO World Heritage Site list and is an important landmark in Nepali tourism. There is no mention of Chitwan – another World Heritage Site in the region.

There are 15 samples of Nepali music in the music gallery of the CD-ROM. All the music is hill folk music and hill traditional songs. But the most revealing fact is that one of the music items in the gallery is a 'Tibetan Wind' album. The use of Tibetan cultural markers in Nepali tourism is nothing new. The major tourism districts in Kathmandu, Pokhara, or Chitwan are flooded with books, paintings, music, and other cultural markers of Tibet. It is recorded by some scholars that Nepal is very keen to use Tibetan icons to promote its tourism (Teague, 1997). The case of Tibetan music in the CD-ROM further proves this point. What is noteworthy here is that the state agency, which has a wider responsibility of representing the country, is borrowing a foreign culture and portraying an inauthentic picture in the CD-ROM. There is another similar example according to a participant, 'Nepal's stalls in international travel and tourism fairs abroad are designed and decorated with Tibetan cultural markers and the Buddhist prayer flags, *Thanka* paintings and *Jhallers*'. The NTB organises Nepal's participation in travel trade shows and when asked about this a participant suggested,

> This is due to the closeness between Tibetan culture and Buddhism, and also that Himalayan heritage of Nepal bears a close resemblance to Tibetan heritage. He said that for this reason the local people residing in and around Lumbini, who are not Buddhist, are never represented in any references to Lumbini.

There is an impressive slide-show presentation in the CD-ROM that features all the prominent tourism activities available in Nepal. It contains a total of 77 photos and five videos, of which 17 are on general tourism themes, 14 are on nature, 19 on culture, 27 on adventure, and 14 on hospitality. There are five videos that are all on adventure themes. The photos and videos all feature mountain-based tourism activities, and there is no reference to any Terai-based tourism resources in the entire presentation.

Why is the region of Terai under-represented in the entire tourism imagery of Nepal? The most obvious answer is that Nepal has always been imaged as a Himalayan Shangri-La and that its touristic identity is based on Himalayan heritage, which is radically different to the imagery of the region of Terai. Some respondents attributed the primacy of Himalayan heritage in Nepal's tourism imagery to be the product of branding, but the question remains why such an all-encompassing brand was chosen. Buzinde, Santos, and Smith (2006) argue that the issue of racial representations presented by tourism is much more than just an image problem, as it holds complex socio-political implications. It is an issue ingrained in history and ideologies, and it is omnipresent in contemporary societies. This suggests to us that the framing of Nepal's tourism identity on Himalayan heritage is informed by the discourse of Nepali nationalism, which correlates Nepaliness with hill identity. Since the cultural heritage of Terai is akin to North Indian heritage it would be of great interest to Indian tourists; but as Indians still are not fully regarded as tourists the development of the *Madhesi* heritage for touristic consumption does not take preference.

The selection of one cultural heritage over another conveys the complicated nature of Nepali identity, which largely is a product of ideology adopted by earlier regimes and despite the cultural diversity of Nepali society. Sharma (2004) believed that the idea of cultural diversity has been a part of and is implicit in Nepal's historical legacy, but this idea of cultural diversity fell short of actually embracing cultural pluralism as a positive value, and the contribution by the people of Terai in the process of nation building has always been undervalued (Sharma, 2004). Adhikary (1998) also views the character of Nepali nationalism as exclusionary, neglecting to incorporate the linguistic communities of Terai. This has happened because the building blocks of common identity were a sense of belonging to the hills rather than the plains, shared cultural characteristics, the Nepali language, and loyalty to the state and to the dynasty that founded it (Whelpton, 2005). This feeling, according to Whelpton, excluded in particular the people of Terai.

Design of Visit Nepal 2020 logo

In April 2018, the Nepali Tourism Minister announced that Nepal would celebrate the year 2020 as a Visit Nepal year. This was a second such initiative in the last 20 years. The first Visit Nepal year was organised in 1998. The background for organising Visit Nepal in 1998 was a number of reasons that included, amongst others, (a) a changed political scenario, as Nepal had a new constitution; (b) strong pursuance of neo-liberal policies and the urge to open the tourism sector to private investors; and (c) the need to enhance the image of Nepal by repositioning it as a unique visitor destination. Since 1998, there have been two other unsuccessful initiatives attempted: one in 2002–2003 as the Destination Nepal campaign and the second in 2011 as Nepal Tourism Year.

The story behind the initiation of the Destination Nepal 2002–2003 campaign is interesting. According to an observer, the campaign was driven by politics at the Ministry of Tourism and Civil Aviation: in December 1998 the government established the Nepal Tourism Board because of intense pressure from the Asian Development Bank, as part of Nepal's commitment to neo-liberal principles – advocated by the bank. The bank had provided a large loan to improve tourism infrastructure in the country, and one of the loan conditions of the bank was that after the Board was formed, the Government would dissolve the Department of Tourism under the Ministry of Tourism and Civil Aviation. After the establishment of the Nepal Tourism Board, all promotional duties were transferred to the NTB. This brought about a huge frustration in the ministry because the high-ranking civil servants in the ministry who enjoyed the frequent foreign travel opportunities associated with tourism promotional campaigns were left with a very limited tourism promotional role. The idea of the Destination Nepal 2002–2003 campaign came about as a way to shore up the ministry's role in tourism promotion and create opportunities for foreign travel in the name of tourism promotion. The unfriendly relationship between the NTB and the ministry leadership further encouraged ministry officials to design the campaign. In essence, the intent of the Destination Nepal campaign was to challenge the NTB's role in international tourism promotion and create foreign traveller opportunities for high-ranking civil servants in the ministry. Thus, the operational format of the Destination Nepal 2002–2003 campaign was that high-ranking civil servants at the ministry would act as coordinators and lead each committee. There were at least four to five foreign visits for each coordinator as part of the campaign. The role of the NTB was kept to a minimum. However, before the campaign could take off, the leadership at the ministry was changed, resulting in a lack of leadership over the campaign within the ministry. Though the Destination Nepal campaign did take off, it could not achieve its objectives because of lack of ownership of the campaign both at the ministry and in the tourism industry. An observer confirmed that petty interests of high-ranking civil servants at the ministry drove the whole campaign. He stated,

> The Visit Nepal 1998 was run through committees because there was no separate promotional body then. It was during this time that need for a separate promotional body was felt and the NTB was created on the last day of Visit Nepal Year so that it could take forward the legacy. Using the Visit Nepal Year 1998 format after the creation of NTB was just driven by the nefarious intentions of the higher civil servants who wanted to increase the opportunities for their foreign travel.

There is a higher allegiance to 'state' nationalism amongst civil servants in Nepal. They predominantly belong to a higher caste group and its 'uniform cultural traits' on which Nepal national identity was created; most of them still follow the traits of the former *Panchayati* regime. For example, many of them were seen in the 'unitary dress code' in their offices even after the government had expanded the narrow definition of dress code to include clothes worn by minority and ethnic groups. A respondent opined that 'national dress' is used by the government officials to impose authority over the 'subjects', as the 'national dress' was used by former royalists to show their allegiance and loyalty to the monarch during the *Panchayati* regime. Because of a strong association with the *Panchayati* regime and its association with royalist supporters 'national dress' was abolished by the government in 2011 after the declaration of the country as a federal republic. The dress was reinstated in August 2018. The stronger allegiance of higher civil servants to the old version of Nepali identity can also be witnessed in the process of the design of the new logo for the proposed Visit Nepal Year 2020.

The Nepal Tourism Board opened a logo competition with the requirement that the logo must contain the tagline 'Lifetime Experiences'. According to the administrator responsible for the logo competition, it should have a unique and vibrant design which successfully conveys the culture and ethos of Nepal, along with its natural, cultural, and religious diversity. The board received 145 entries altogether. A small NTB team consisting of external experts on logo design selected the best five logos and forwarded them for consideration to a logo selection committee consisting of the Minister for Tourism and Civil Aviation, the chief executive officer at the NTB, and tourism industry and association representatives. The committee made the final selection, and the minister unveiled the logo through his Facebook page. An officer who was associated with the logo selection process informed me that Facebook was deliberately chosen so that they could get an immediate response from the public and, if needed, changes could be made. He states,

> We used social media to make the design public because we wanted to see what comments people would make. Our intention was to get feedback from members of the public and see if there were any genuine elements missing or misrepresented.

He also believed that the logo was contemporary and very well represented the sociocultural fabric of Nepal. This was the general impression amongst those involved in the selection of the logo. Uploading the logo on her Facebook page, a manager at the NTB who was also involved in the selection process posted,

> The logo truly depicts Nepal's ethos and vibes and stands true to the message; 'Visit Nepal for Lifetime Experiences'. The logo will be used as the main promotional branding of the #VNY2020 Campaign.

Interestingly, there were immediate comments on her Facebook post challenging the logo, particularly its unrepresentativeness and inappropriateness. For example, one comment stated, 'Promotional Logo for Nepal must depict Himalayas, Buddha, Safari (Wildlife) and Rich Cultural Features, and (for me) this logo only covers the Himalayas'. Another commented, 'Everest should stand alone not with fishtail. There is no ethnic vibes and varieties of culture, geography in the (first) logo'. Another comment stated

Figure 3.1a Visit Nepal 2020

'The mountains are wrongly placed. At least in Nepalese eyes. And it does not speak anything about Lord Buddha!'

Comments also came through other mediums, such as text messages and telephone calls. According to the NTB officer, the main contention in the originally selected design concerned the mountain. The two mountains in the logo background are Mt. Everest and Fishtail. The comments mainly criticised the prominence given to Fishtail over Mt. Everest. A commentator said,

> Even if you look geographically the Himalayan mountain range are spread along Nepal's northern side from east to west. Mt Everest is in the eastern side and Fishtail is on the west from it. Therefore, in the logo Mt Everest should come first and then Fishtail.

The above comment is important. Mt. Everest is an international icon and a heritage of 'universal' value. To Nepal, the home of the mountain, it has wider economic, social, cultural meanings: it is the lifeline of mountain tourism; it embodies Nepali nationhood and reinforces a sense of identity. For example, Mt. Everest became a unanimous choice when, after the monarchy was suspended in 2006, the central bank of Nepal began searching for a replacement for the king's images on Nepali bank notes. Mt. Everest has achieved an added importance because of the recent disasters in the Everest region, such as the 2014 avalanche and the April 2015 earthquake, which killed many people in the area of the mountain. These incidents have exposed the fragility of the Himalayan mountains, demystifying the view that they are indomitable, the character for which Mt. Everest has been associated in the existence of the Nepali nation. Given such a background, the iconic significance of Mt. Everest in the psyche of common Nepalis cannot be overlooked.

However, mountains also symbolise the contested side of Nepali national identity that is largely dominated by the cultural landscape of the highlands, overlooking the other provincial heritages of the nation. There is a big contention over the over-emphasis on Mt. Everest in Nepal's tourism landscape, and the Fishtail could have been chosen because the current Minister of Tourism comes from the region whose economy depends largely on tourism activities in and around the Fishtail mountain. Some commentators also expressed disagreement with the mountain imagery in the design. For example, a commentator stated,

> What a cheap design selection by NTB, How they will make branding and promotion even not show any glimpse of unity in the Diversity. I am not arguing but the logo has to give deep meaning . . .

Similarly, another commentator stated,

> Not even a small glimpse of a World Heritage Site is there . . . It seems only Himalayas are enough, culture is there, tradition is there but it would have been even (more) better if small trace of the uniqueness of Nepal's Stupa, Temple, Durbar Square, World Heritage Site is seen.

Because of the huge criticism of the logo in the first few days on social media, the authorities made some important changes in the original design, and the final logo was unveiled after three days. The main issues were with: (a) the position of Mt Everest, (b) the prominence of the Nepali flag in the logo, and (c) the use of the lower case for Nepal. The government made these changes, and the logo was finally unveiled the second time (see Figure 3.1).

Figure 3.1b Visit Nepal 2020

These changes however, did not incorporate the issues of the lack of Nepal's cultural diversity in the logo as expressed by some commentators above. The author tried to get some deeper understanding of the design and the process of selection from the tourism industry. Most of them agreed with the comments that it fails to represent the ethnic and cultural diversity of Nepal. For example, a participant said,

> Nepal is a multi-ethnic country and there is greater diversity of heritage and cultural practices. However, if you see the logo, this is dominated by traditional imagery that rested in the culture of the valley (Kathmandu valley) and the mountains. It does not show the Terai plains where there is diverse culture and more than half of the population lives.

There are other comments that showed how the representation in the logo becomes a playground for the articulation of Nepali nationhood. The most prominent arose over the low profile given to the Nepali flag in the first design. This is interesting because the use of the national flag in tourism representation has not received enough attention. A participant said,

> We have a unique flag and this should be more prominently placed in the logo. Nepal is the only country in the world that does not have a rectangular national flag. It is crimson with blue borders and incorporates stylized symbols of the sun and moon. The flag also symbolizes the victory in war by the great warriors of *Nepal*. The blue border denotes the peace in the country.

There is great significance of the national flag in the articulation of nationalism because of its rich symbolic and political connotations, its long history, its ubiquity, and its emotional power. Most theorists of nationalism refer to flags as a pillar of nationhood, along with other institutions. Billig (1995) describes the ubiquity of the use of the national flag in the United States, the United Kingdom, and New Zealand as creeping 'banal' nationalism. The basic difference between these nations and unestablished nations, on the symbolic level, Billig claims, is one between 'the flag hanging unnoticed on the public building' and 'a flag which is being consciously waved with fervent passion' (Billig, 1995, p. 8). Massive and fervent flag waving certainly takes place in the United States as well these days, more so than in many other states. However, some scholars do take a critical view of the flag and believe that in insecure nations flags and other national symbols often fail to fulfil their most important function as promoters of national unity (Eriksen and Jenkins, 2007).

Kolsto (2006) also takes the view that in weak and insecure nations flags and other national symbols often fail to fulfil their most important function as promoters of national unity: he is of the opinion that they instead bring to the fore strong divisions within the putative nation. However, despite going through tumultuous political upheavals in recent years, the position of the Nepali national flag has remained very strong, though not uncontested in Nepal. There was a minor voice in the Constituent Assembly by the then-Maoist Party to change the national flag during the discussion on the new republic constitution, which was very strongly opposed by other political parties and civil society representatives: the proposal was withdrawn without much discussion in the assembly. In the discussion on the Visit Nepal logo, it appeared that people consider the Nepali flag more than a cultural symbol. A participant stated,

> Our flag is not only our official representation but it is also a part of our lifestyle. We have cultural and religious significance with the flag, for example, we keep them in temples or religious ceremonies. You will see them during festivals. Our flag has been one of the important things that keeps us united. So if we want this (VNY 2020) to be a national campaign, it is important that we have our flag in the logo to bring whole Nepalis together.

Conclusions

This chapter has argued that the tourism imagery of Nepal is full of references to Himalayan culture, whereas a region that has its own touristic resources, cultural heritage, and regional identity is largely left out of official tourism representations. The under-representation of the region of Terai in Nepali tourism is the result of the stereotyping of Nepal's tourism identity that relies on the image created of 'Shangri-La' and the continuation of the nationalist mindset of the regime discussed in the previous chapter. This imagery is also informed by the 'nationalist' discourse that was targeted at creating Nepal's distinctiveness compared with India. The above narrative of the Nepali nation in tourism representations has a significance because tourism at one level is a particular experience, such as a museum visit, but at a deeper level it is an intangible idea or feeling, whether fantasy, nostalgia, pleasure, pride, and the like.

The case of the new logo suggests that tourism has been an area in which to articulate and express the nation's cultural identity and assert its distinctiveness. The assertion of national distinctiveness – which is expressed through cultural authenticity and identity – is a form of nationalism, because according to Gellner (1999), nationalism is concerned with using the pre-existing, historically inherited proliferation of cultures or cultural wealth. In the view of Anderson (1991), the assertion of a common sense of identity is important in imagining the nation, to which museums, sacred sites, and monuments can be a medium to create an image of nation and spread the sense of community. However, this does not mean that the narration of nation produced by tourism needs to be consistent or homogenous. There can be a multiplicity of heritage across regions, but we have seen here that there is still a lack of realisation of the above.

If Nepal has to evolve a new national identity, it will have to accommodate vernacular heritage and culture. By under-representing Terai and *Madhesh* in the official touristic representation as shown in this chapter, tourism is producing a version of Nepal which is incomplete. However, there has been increasing engagement with *Madhesh*'s heritage and cultural identity from generic public in more recent years. This has been witnessed in the case of Lumbini, that is still very sparsely represented in official touristic accounts, whereas in the last decade, Lumbini has occupied an important place both in Nepal's national imagery and as a visitor attraction. Representation of a place is about representing its people, culture, and the landscape. However, this was lacking in the case of Lumbini. Until very recently, the image of Buddha dominated the narrative on Lumbini, which was unhelpful, as this aided the exclusion and dislodging of cultural geography of the region in which Lumbini is located. However, the above exclusionary nature of narrative of Lumbini has started change, and Lumbini has started to become more positive in the expression and 'celebration' of Nepali national identity. In the next chapter, we will look at the case of Lumbini in the articulation of Nepali nationalism.

References

Adhikary, D. P. (1998). *History of Nepalese Nationalism*. Kathmandu: Romila Acharya.
Anderson, B. (1991). *Imagined Communities: Reflections on the Origin and Spread of Nationalism*. London: Verso.
Ateljvic, I. and Doorne, S. (2002). Representing New Zealand: Tourism Imagery and Ideology. *Annals of Tourism Research*, 29(3), 648–667.
Billig, M. (1995, 2001). *Banal Nationalism*. London: Sage Publications.
Brown, R. H. (1995). The Poststructural Crisis in the Social Sciences: Learning from James Joyce. In R. H. Brown (Ed.), *Postmodern Representations: Truth, Power and Mimesis in the Human Sciences and Public Culture* (pp. 134–167). Urbana and Chicago: University of Illinois Press.
Butler, R. W. (1990). The Influence of the Media in Shaping International Tourist Patterns. *Tourism Recreation Research*, 15, 46–53.
Butler, R. W. (1998). Tartan Mythology, the Traditional Tourist Image of Scotland. In R. Ringer (Ed.), *Destinations: Cultural Landscape of Tourism* (pp. 121–139). London: Routledge.

Buzinde, C. N., Santos, C. A. and Smith, S. L. J. (2006). Ethnic Representations: Destination Imagery. *Annals of Tourism Research*, 33(3), 707–728.

Chambers, E. (2000). *Native Tours: The Anthropology of Travel and Tourism*. Prospect Heights, IL: Waveland Press.

Eriksen, T. E. and Jenkins, R. (2007). *Flag, Nation and Symbolism in Europe and America*. London: Routledge.

Gaige, F. H. (1975). *Regionalism and National Unity in Nepal*. New Delhi: Vikas Publishing House.

Geertz, C. (1995). *After the Fact: Two Counties, Four Decades, One Anthropologist*. Cambridge, MA: Harvard University Press.

Gellner, E. (1999). *Nations and Nationalism*. Oxford: Blackwell Publishing.

Grandin, I. (1996). 'To Change the Face of This Country' Nepalese Progressive Songs under Panchayat Democracy. *Journal of South Asian Literature*, 29(1), 175–189.

Hall, S. (1996). Who Needs Identity? In S. Hall and P. Gay (Eds.), *Questions of Cultural Identity* (pp. 1–17). London: Sage Publications.

Hepburn, S. J. (2002). Touristic Forms of Life in Nepal. *Annals of Tourism Research*, 29(3), 611–630.

Hollinshead, K. (2000). Representation. In J. Jafari (Ed.), *Encyclopaedia of Tourism* (p. 501). New York: Routledge.

Hunter, W. A. (2008). A Typology of Photographic Representations for Tourism: Depictions of Groomed Spaces. *Tourism Management*, 29, 354–365.

Kolsto, P. (2006). National Symbols as Signs of Unity and Division. *Ethnic and Racial Studies*, 29(4), 676–701.

Lanfant, M. F. (1995). *Introduction*. In M.F. Lanfant, J.B. Allcock and E.M. Bruner (Eds.) International Tourism: Identity and Change (pp. 1–23). London: Sage.

Light, D. (2001). 'Facing the Future': Tourism and Identity-Building in Post-Socialist Romania. *Political Geography*, 20(8), 1053–1074.

MacCannell, D. (1999). *The Tourist a New Theory of the Leisure Class*. Berkeley, CA: University of California Press.

McCrone, D., Morris, A. and Kiely, R. (1995). *Scotland: The Brand the Making of Scottish Heritage*. Edinburgh: Edinburgh University Press.

McLean, F. (2005). Guest Editorial: Museums and National Identity. *Museum and Society*, 3(1), 1–4.

McLean, F. and Cooke, S. (2003). Constructing the Identity of a Nation: The Tourist Gaze at the Museum of Scotland. *Tourism Culture and Communication*, 4(3), 153–162.

Ministry of Culture, Tourism and Civil Aviation (MoTCA). (2016). *Nepal Tourism Statistics (2016)*. Kathmandu: Government of Nepal.

Morgan, N. and Pritchard, A. (1998). *Tourism Promotion and Power: Creating Images, Creating Identities*. Chichester: John Wiley & Sons.

Nepal Tourism Board (NTB) (n.d.a). Nepal Nationalism Ethnographic Mesuem [Brochure].

Nepal Tourism Board (NTB) (n.d.a). Naturally Nepal Once is Not Enough [CDROM].

Pitchford, S. (2006). Identity Tourism: A Medium for Native American Stories. *Tourism Culture and Communication*, 6(2), 85–105.

Pitchford, S. (2008). *Identity Tourism Imaging and Imagining the Nation*. London: Elsevier.

Pretes, M. (2003). Tourism and Nationalism. *Annals of Tourism Research*, 30(1), 125–142.

Ratz, T. and Irimias, A. (2017). Imagine Ben Hur in Formula One: An Analysis of the National Gallop in Hungary. In L. White (Ed.), *Commercial Nationalism and Tourism: Selling the National Story* (pp. 195–211). Bristol: Channel View Publications.

Ryan, C. (2002). Tourism and Cultural Proximity: Examples from New Zealand. *Annals of Tourism Research*, 29, 952–971.

Sharma, P. R. (2004). *The State and the Society in Nepal*. Kathmandu: Himal Books.

Sharma, P. R. (2012). Some Aspects of Nepal's Social Demography: Update 2011. *Studies in Nepali History and Society*, 17(2), December.

Smith, A. D. (1999). *Myths and Memories of the Nation*. Oxford: Oxford University Press.

Smith, A. D. (2009). *Ethno-Symbolism and Nationalism: A Cultural Approach*. New York: Routledge.

Teague, K. (1997). Representations of Nepal. In S. Abram, J. Waldren and D. V. MacLeod (Eds.), *Tourists and Tourism: Identifying with People and Places* (pp. 173–195). Oxford: Berg.

Urry, J. (2006). *The Tourist Gaze*. London: Sage Publications.

Whelpton, J. (2005). *A History of Nepal*. Cambridge: Cambridge University Press.

White, L. (2017). *Commercial Nationalism and Tourism: Selling the National Story*. Bristol: Channel View Publications.

Zolberg, V. L. (1996). Museums as Contested Sites of Remembrance. In S. Macdonald and G. Fyfe (Eds.), *Theorising Museums* (pp. 69–82). Oxford: Black Publishers and The Sociological Review.

4   Expressing nationalism at Lumbini

Lumbini is a UNESCO-listed world heritage site and an important icon of Nepali national identity. This chapter takes the case of Lumbini heritage to examine how Nepali visitors identify themselves with Lumbini and use it to assert Nepal's autonomy and independence. I argue that the strong collective sentiment associated with Lumbini serves as an opportunity for Nepali visitors to reassert a boundary with the 'Other' of Nepali nationalism. The chapter investigates the narrative of Nepali visitors about their feelings in visiting the Lumbini heritage and it also examines the intersections between tourism and nationalism when a Chinese NGO proposed a project to invest $3 billion to develop it as a heritage tourism hub. The strong opposition to the project highlights the collaboration between tourism and Nepali nationalism in defending Lumbini from the 'perceived' invasion into the heritage that has very lately acquired a special place in Nepal's collective identity.

However, it is imperative to begin this chapter by providing a brief outline of Lumbini. Lumbini is the birthplace of Gautama Buddha. The place was very little known until the late 19th century (Bidari, 2004), when in 1896, a group of archaeologists rediscovered it. The site was not properly looked after until the United Nations General Secretary visited it in 1967. In 1972, a Japanese architect, Kenzo Tange, was hired by the United Nations Development Programme to prepare a master plan for the development and preservation of the site. With global interest and the importance of Lumbini, the UNESCO World Heritage Commission named Lumbini a World Heritage Site in 1997. The Nepal Tourism Board, has been promoting tourism in Lumbini rigorously in all international travel trade shows as any other mass tourism destination. Though this is somehow contradictory because such promotional endeavours are focussed on development and commercialisation, UNESCO avoids over-development based on the master plan (Nyaupane, 2009).

The reason for choosing Lumbini was because Lumbini is the biggest visitor attraction in Nepal and receives a total of more than 1.5 million visitors annually, of which 1.2 million are Nepalis (Anmol, 2018). In terms of international visitors, Lumbini received 136,000 visitors in 2016, excluding Indian tourists (MoTCA, 2016). More than 134,000 Indian tourists visited Lumbini that year. Another reason for choosing Lumbini is because Buddhism forms an important aspect of Nepali culture and is a very important selling point for Nepali tourism. However, for the majority of Nepali Hindus, 'pilgrimage' usually only refers to visits to Hindu religious sites, and the role of Buddhist shrines or pilgrimage in their self-identification has not been very well known. Furthermore, Lumbini evoked a very strong nationalist sentiment when a Chinese project was proposed to develop it as a tourist hub. It would be illuminating to see how Nepalis understand and associate themselves with Lumbini and the innate values it evokes for them.

Heritage, geopolitics, and nationalism

Heritage is concerned with the preservation and representation of values (Hall and Jenkins, 1995). Nation-states have deployed heritage to project a desired narrative of a nation and the values it represents, sometimes through manipulation or coercion and at other times through genuine efforts of heritage conservation. Thus, the construction of heritage is not determined by resource endowment alone but is largely subject to interpretation, which is processed through mythology, ideology, nationalism, local pride, and other factors (Schouten, 1995). As a result, heritage often becomes an emblem of its national culture, fraught with contestation and conflict when different groups compete in the production of heritage narratives. If a heritage has transnational significance, the contestation can spill over national boundaries.

Heritage plays a huge part in the construction and regulation of meaning and understandings and embodies a discourse (Smith, 2006). The message at a heritage site can reflect social meanings, relations, and entities; however, such meaning may not always be independently formed. It is often guided by the power relations underlying the discourse, which dictates those who have the authority to 'speak' about or 'for' heritage and those who do not (Smith, 2006). Because of such ramifications of heritage, it is regarded as a social construction (Hall and Jenkins, 1995). Another factor in the above role of heritage is the designation of UNESCO World Heritage Site status. The new status can speed up the process of social construction by creating institutions to manage and aid the development of heritage. This is helpful in the use-value of heritage, but it can also downplay and depoliticise local heritage practices and may discourage the universalism and rootedness of local practices by overemphasising the singularity of the concept of universal value (Tucker and Carnegie, 2014). Furthermore, World Heritage status

also elevates heritage sites to the status of global icon and national trea-
sure (Smith, 2006), raising their symbolic value and transforming them into
icons of history and culture. On many occasions the promotion of tourism
relies on such iconic stature. Tourism is often charged with the allegations
of exploiting and mobilising heritage as a political tool to represent the
desired ideology of the country, promoting official nationalism. Robinson
and Smith (2006) argue that nations promote heritage tourism as a marker of
political status, drawing upon cultural capital as a means to legitimise itself
as a territorial entity (Robinson and Smith, 2006).

There are numerous cases that show the symbiotic relationship between
heritage and nationalism (Aitchison, 1999; Graham, Ashworth and Tunbridge, 2000). For example, French sociologist Lanfant (1995) acknowledges the role of heritage in depicting 'nationness' through a forging of
signs of identity: for instance, memorable places, historic monuments, the
heritage of traditional societies, and craft skills. However, such a process
of heritage creation is very selective and on many occasions a cause for
concern, because it could lead to a feeling of exclusion to some heritage
communities (see Graham, 2002). In such cases, designation of heritage
status can result in the denial of identity. This was strongly suggested in
Lumbini because the proposed project exemplified the perception that any
Chinese or Indian engagement in Lumbini would mean the renunciation of
Nepali identity. Nepali national identification is not formed independently,
but it is strongly informed by the nation's interaction with and perception
of the external 'Other'. Because of this, considerable reference is made to
external elements in the articulation of Nepali national identity (see Bhandari, 2016). Gellner (2016) agrees to a similar notion of Nepal being an
'interface' between two major cultural areas to the north and south, referring
to China and India. This brings in the strong presence of a geopolitical ingredient in the expression of Nepali nationalism. Since geopolitics is concerned
with how contingencies of various geopolitical actors and processes shape
the dynamics of interstate relations, it is imperative to consider this in the
case discussed here.

Traditionally, geopolitics focussed on the state's ability to make others do
your will, often through military force; however, the concept now includes
state-directed economic pressures. Scholars have identified such tactics as
'hard' and 'soft' geopolitics, where in the former type, states use militarism,
organised violence, and war to competitively acquire, control, and defend
territory. In the latter case, states employ competitive and coercive interactions, using political-economic tactics to exercise and increase their political
clout and maximise their individual economic gain (see Kraxberger and
McClaughry, 2013). West II (2006) believes that the focus of contemporary geopolitics is on the dynamics of 'power to' produce things, induce

pleasure, form knowledge, or produce discourse. It takes an interest in how the dynamics of power or knowledge are woven through the way geopolitical actors represent and contest material spatial practices. Thus, the domain of geopolitics includes the value, importance, and effect of the political and economic programmes of states or international institutions on geopolitical representations.

One of the ways such geopolitical goals are achieved is through the discourse of 'development' and 'aid'. For example, following the Cuban revolution in 1959 there was a dramatic increase in US interest in Latin America in the context of a growing concern that the USSR was gaining ground in the Third World. As part of its wider emphasis on foreign aid and national development, the Kennedy administration formed the Peace Corps in 1961 and then set up the US Agency for International Development (USAID) to coordinate and combine government foreign aid initiatives (Berger, 2006). Though different in design, the Chinese project described below would still exemplify how the heritage of Buddhism can manifest political geographic structures to reproduce positions of power in the region, which is one of the main purposes of geopolitics. Scholars of critical geopolitics agree that expressions of geographical difference contribute to a politics of identity formation (Dodds, 2005). Thus, the proposed investment plan in Lumbini would not only bring China closer to the Indian border but also create a critical mass that views China as a bastion of Buddhism. Interestingly, studies on the geopolitics of 'global' heritage sites are still lacking: most of those that exist are on the 'politics of heritage', focussed on contestation, dissonance, and conflict (Naef and Ploner, 2016), which is surprising, given that regional and international geopolitics do affect the proceedings of the World Heritage Committee when it is considering UNESCO World Heritage Site status (Meskell, Liuzza, Bertacchini and Saccone, 2015).

Lumbini in Nepali national imagination

The assimilation of Buddhists or Buddhism in the 'national' narrative is still very recent in Nepal. Buddhism was in the past merely mentioned as an important part of Nepali culture, but the actual integration of it into the national iconography was within a larger Hindu value system, and Buddhists did not enjoy equal status and power in social and political spheres in Nepal. Tewari (1983) argues that since the 13th century Buddhism has been waning and losing its vigour because of the ascendancy of Hinduism. Tewari considers that the process of its decline started during the mediaeval period but accelerated after the advent of the Shah dynasty in the latter half of the 18th century. Though Shah rulers followed a policy of accommodation and tolerance towards Buddhism to some extent, this policy received a setback with the rise of the Ranas in the mid-19th century, who relentlessly pursued a policy of vigorous Hinduisation. It was only after the end of the Rana regime in 1951, followed by the establishment of democracy in Nepal, that a policy of liberalisation was instituted by the state and a more favourable atmosphere was created for Buddhists.

Until the early 1990s Lumbini never received any attention from the Nepali state for two reasons. First, Nepal took pride in being the only Hindu kingdom in the world, and all state machineries were mobilised to maintain this status. Other religions that did not comply with the larger national narrative of Hinduism either became part of it or were never included in the Nepali national imagery. Though it was not constitutionally defined as such, Buddhism was viewed as part of Hinduism. Such practice could have been influenced by neighbouring Indian states, where Buddhism was legislatively incorporated as a part of Hinduism (Chaudhary, 2011). There was also another geopolitical issue with Lumbini, though this is more concerned with Nepali national identity. Geographically, Lumbini is in the southern plains, the region close to India. We have noted in Chapter 3 that in the common Nepali mindset, the people and culture of the southern plains were imagined as the 'Other'. This was because of their cultural proximity to India (Gaige, 1975), and as a result Lumbini did not make a mark as a national icon. However, this has started to change after the adaptation to parliamentary democracy. Furthermore, the designation of the World Heritage Site (WHS) status has raised the profile of Lumbini considerably so that Nepal's national iconography is now incomplete without the Buddha and Lumbini.

The popularity of Lumbini and its association with Nepal's national identity has been boosted by a number of factors in recent years. The foremost is the development of Buddhist heritage tours in the northern Indian states. This has been perceived as a threat and a marginalisation of Lumbini. Some participants believed that India is also developing a 'fake' Lumbini on the Indian side as per 'their' plan to revive the ancient Nalanda civilisation. In reaction to India's development of Buddhist circuits close to Lumbini on the Indian side of the border, the government of Nepal decided to celebrate 2012 as Visit Lumbini Year 2012. A participant thought that it was necessary to have such a nationalist response to India's Buddhism plans. In the opinion of the Minister for Culture, the campaign was aimed at promoting Lumbini to the international community and inviting national and international tourists. However, one participant claimed that the campaign was a case of nationalist reaction against the perennial Indian reference to India as the birthplace of Lord Buddha.

Any reference by India that challenges Buddha's birthplace has been refuted more strongly since Nepal became religiously secular in 2008 through the republican constitution. For example, in 2009 a Bollywood movie allegedly said Buddha was born in India, which was strongly protested against by student bodies of Communist parties, forcing the government to ban it from screening. The government called the misrepresentation in the film an attack on Nepal's nationalism (TOI, 2009) and defended its position by saying, 'Our censor board had struck out the controversial comments in the film before approving it for screening. But considering the popular sentiments, we have banned it' (Reuters, 2009). Expressions of Nepali nationalism have been intensively pursued through tourism promotional campaigns. A participant confirmed that the Visit Lumbini Year of 2012 was directed towards India's smear campaign against Lumbini. Since 2012, the Nepali Tourist Board has been more conspicuous in representing Lumbini in travel trade shows. For example, when the researcher visited the Nepal stand in the World Travel Mart (WTM) in London in 2012, Lumbini as the Birthplace was its central theme. However, in terms of representation of Lumbini in its regular tourism outlets such as websites, printed brochures, and promotional CD-ROMs, Lumbini does not feature prominently despite increasing numbers of visitors in more recent years. A member of the Nepal delegation at WTM confirmed that the reference to Lumbini in the stand was to protect Lumbini from India's 'offensive', suggesting that it does not into see Lumbini as a star attraction in itself.

The appropriateness of using the Buddha in tourism promotion can be a contentious issue, though this has not received enough attention in Nepal. There are examples of states that have been reticent in according their heritage global stature if such heritage involved religions (Graham, Ashworth and Tunbridge, 2000). Some participants took the view that Hindus have deliberately denigrated the Buddhist shrine by promoting it as a tourist attraction. This has happened because on many occasions there is no proper Buddhist representation in their governing bodies. A Buddhist participant questioned, 'Can you expect a non-Hindu to head the Pashupati Area Development Trust? So why should a Hindu head a committee to develop Buddha's birthplace?' Lack of a Nepali Buddhist monk representation was very conspicuous when the government formed a six-member Lumbini Development National Directive Committee under UCPN-Maoist Chairman Prachanda. A participant said, 'With Nepal's transition to secularism we had expected that our rights will be protected, but Prachanda's appointment is an indication that things have not changed'. The claims of religious and cultural incongruity in heritage representation are not new and have happened in other places. For example, the Mahabodhi Vihara, one of the biggest Buddhist sites for pilgrimage in India, has been fighting to establish Buddhist control of their heritage from Hindus (Chaudhary, 2011).

Scholars have noted that heritage is ideologically connected with nationalist sentiment (Lowenthal, 1998). It is concerned 'with the ways in which very selective material artefacts, mythologies, memories and traditions become resources for the present' (Graham, 2002, p. 1004). According to Graham (2002), the landscapes of heritage and tourism consumption are simultaneously other people's sacred places, and dissonance arises because of the zero-sum characteristics of heritage, all of which belongs to someone and logically, therefore, not to someone else. Ashworth (1997, p. 12) states that, 'if all heritage by being someone's, must disinherit someone else, then a world heritage is not a happy summation of local and national heritage, but rather a denial of them'. The sentiment in Nepal over international interests in Lumbini has exemplified this attitude, as any Chinese or Indian engagement in Lumbini would mean the denial of Nepal's national identity. A similar consequence has also been evident in proposed projects in hydropower and highways. For example, the government's desire to contract an Indian company to construct a fast-track highway to the capital, Kathmandu, received huge opposition in 2016.

Expressing Nepali nationalism at Lumbini

The author also visited the Lumbini heritage site on three separate occasions between 2013 and 2018 to see how people perform Nepali nationalism at the site. Visitors are seen flocking in groups from the very early morning throughout the day. The main place where Buddha was born is inside the *Mayadevi* temple. Nepali visitors were seen entering the temple in the early morning and were trying to perform 'puja', a prayer ritual of devotional worship to deities, as they would do in a Hindu temple. However, visitors are not allowed to perform any *puja* inside the *Mayadevi* temple. There were people queuing for lighting lamps and incense in the nearby *Pipal* (sacred fig) tree next to the temple. When asked why they were performing puja, many visitors took the view that Buddha is the incarnation of lord Vishnu, and they wanted to perform the puja as they would do in a Vishnu temple:

> I am a follower of Vishnu. Since, Buddha is an avatar of Lord Vishnu, I wanted to pay homage to Vishnu. Though I could not offer puja inside the temple, I am happy to light candles and offer flowers in the *Pipal* tree.

There were visitors wearing clothes that they would normally use when visiting a Hindu pilgrimage in India. Other visitors' clothes were full of imprinted images of Nepal's national symbols, Mt. Everest, or the Nepali national flag. Since the area covered by the heritage site is extremely large, it is a usual sight to see people spending time taking selfies and family pictures, and it has also become a place for picnics. There was an entire village community travelling together to Lumbini. For example, a group from western Nepal had hired a minibus to visit the place. A visitor in his mid-fifties was seen taking a selfie with a Nepali flag in one hand. When asked about this, he explained,

> I brought this Nepali flag to take a picture here, because Buddha is one of our biggest icons and I feel proud to be present here. For me coming to Lumbini is one of the ways to see where the country's biggest son was born. I wanted to capture this moment with a national flag in my hand. Additionally, I am very impressed with the maintenance and general cleanliness of this place.

Another visitor took out a Nepali cap just before taking his selfie. He stated that he wanted to look more Nepali before taking this picture so that Buddha and his Nepaliness is captured in the picture. He said,

> See Buddha is one of world's biggest icons. It is our privilege that he was born in Nepal. However, we all know that India is trying to fake the world that Buddha belonged to India and was born there. In visiting this place and seeing the development here I am really proud of my country. It is one of the very few places where donning a Nepali cap makes you feel pride.

This is interesting, because the historicity of the nation has always been debated. However, it is worth noting that probably there was no Nepali nation at the time of Buddha; however, there is a strong assertion of Buddha's Nepali nationality, at least in Nepal's national narratives in recent years. Lumbini has become such an intense national symbol that when the Tibetan religious leader the Dalai Lama argued that Buddha did not belong to one nation, this created great resentment in Nepal. The Dalai Lama's argument was that in ancient times there were no separate countries that we know today, and many countries of South Asia, for example, Nepal, India, China, Vietnam, Laos, and some republics in Russia, were part of the Mahabharata. In this sense, according to the Dalai Lama, 'Buddha was a great Indian master of Asia' (Republica, 2017). However, this statement met huge criticism in Nepal, where the Dharmodaya Sabha (national Buddhist Association of Nepal) urged him to stop spreading such misleading information about the birthplace of Gautama Buddha (Republica, 2017). The Sabha stated that even the UN has recognised Nepal as the birthplace of Buddha and enlisted the place in the World Heritage list. Due to huge resentment over his remarks, the Dalai Lama later clarified that his intent was misunderstood and accepted that Lord Buddha was born in Lumbini in today's Nepal.

Interestingly, some of the visitors to Lumbini were aware of the Dalai Lama's statement: a participant stated that it has become more imperative for all Nepalis to visit Lumbini and spread the message that Buddha was born in Nepal. He stated,

> We should declare Lumbini a national pilgrimage. Out of our two global icons, Mt. Everest is too tall and difficult to reach for common Nepalis. However, Lumbini is accessible to anyone and can be visited irrespective of their faith, unlike Pashupatinath which is only open for Hindus. Buddha's message of peace, harmony and coexistence is very much relevant to all Nepalis in the changed political context of Nepal where ex-Maoists fighters have been assimilated into the society. It is equally important to us as a country.

The above comments conform to the earlier findings by Park (2011) that heritage is a major emblem of nationhood and lies at the core of legitimising the existence of the nation and maintaining the nation's unique and exclusive qualities. The visitors at Lumbini were quite conscious of the place of Lumbini in Nepali national imagination and its role vis-à-vis other icons of Nepali national identity. Notably, not all visitors who came to Lumbini were interested in its sacredness or the place where he was born. Though they all visited the *Mayadevi* temple where the sacrosanct or the holy of holies is located, visitors were there mainly for the reason that Lumbini is a special place for them. A participant said,

> The entire Lumbini heritage site is one of its kinds in the country. I feel proud to be Nepali when I come here. It represents the spirit of Nepal and the Nepali people which is based on Buddha's philosophy of peace and *panchasheela*.

The comments above by visitors reiterate the point that for those Nepalis visiting Lumbini, it is more than a World heritage site, it epitomises the Nepali nation. It is not unusual for a tourism or heritage site to play such a role. For example, Franklin (2003) suggests that tourism can become an integral part of national life through which people experience the idea of nationhood and collective past. A similar view is expressed by Palmer (1999) who regards heritage tourism as having a role in the maintenance and promotion of the nation. According to Palmer, heritage tourism enables people to conceive, imagine, and confirm their belonging to the nation (Palmer, 1999). She asserts that visits to heritage settings are expected to encourage nationals to feel part of and connected to the nation's past in their national imagination. The above expressions of the visitors at the Lumbini heritage site suggest that similar outcome, that Lumbini plays a significant role in imagining the essence of Nepali national identity. It has also shown that Lumbini is not perceived as a mere remnant of the past, but it is seen as a symbolic embodiment of past and an important element in the iconography of collective memories or shared values in society that plays a part in enhancing the group's social and cultural identities. This is what Bessière (1998, p. 26) identifies as the role of heritage. He asserts:

> Heritage, whether it be an object, monument, inherited skill or symbolic representation, must be considered as an identity marker and distinguishing feature of a social group. Heritage is often a subjective element because it is directly related to a collective social memory . . . social memory as a common legacy preserves the cultural and social identity of a given community, through more or less ritualized circumstances.
>
> (Bessière, 1998, p. 26 cited in Park, 2010, p. 119)

The contest for Buddhism

In 2011, a Chinese non-governmental organisation named the Asia Pacific Economic Cooperation and Exchange Foundation (APECEF) came up with a proposal to invest three billion US$ in Lumbini, the birthplace of Gautama Buddha, aimed at making it a 'Mecca for Buddhists' (The Economist, 2011). The plan included building an airport, hotels, convention centres, a highway, Buddhist temples and a Buddhist university in Lumbini and was backed by Nepal's Maoist Communist Party. The proposal received wider condemnation in the international media, especially the Indian media that labelled it a Chinese design to hijack Buddha, the 'fountain of Buddhism'. In Nepal, it drew considerable public interest and was seen as an encroachment on its national identity and that the proposal undermined long-standing cooperation with the UN agency, UNESCO, to implement the already existing Lumbini Master Plan.

There is a view that India and China are in competition with each other across Asia (Scott, 2008; Reeves, 2012). Scholars argue that India and China have 'widening geopolitical horizons' and that 'they both strive to stamp their authority on the same region' (also see Fuller and Arguilla, 1996; Malik, 2004). According to Scott (2008), the Himalayas pose a formidable barrier to military adventurism in either direction. But situated in between the giant countries, Nepal assumes an importance in a geopolitical sense, in particular since China's direct hold on Tibet since 1950. China has built up its military presence in Tibet, and permanent long-distance highways and railway lines have been constructed, which is an indication of China's anxiety about Tibet (Scott, 2008). A top Chinese expert confirmed such worries when writing in a state-controlled newspaper in China that China's infrastructural superiority in the Tibet Autonomous Region will likely come under pressure from India's high growth in the coming years (THT, 2016). In the eyes of the media the main contention about the project lies in the India–China competition in the region. For instance, an influential Nepali daily newspaper that detailed an analysis of the Lumbini 'controversy' viewed that the project was trapped in the India–China rivalry, with many media accusing China of instigating a geopolitical race in Nepal. For example, a commentator wrote,

> How deeply are the Chinese Government and the Communist Party of China involved with the APECEF proposal, or is this a renegade operation? The project document lists an entity of the Chinese Ministry of Commerce as the 'government co-ordinating agency'. With Lumbini's heritage sites less than 4 km from the Indian border at its closest, does the project hold out the danger of raising a reaction from India and triggering geopolitical competition that would harm Nepali interests?
>
> (Dixit, 2011)

Upadhya (2012) contends that China's geo-strategic interest in Nepal is not unfounded, and from the Chinese perspective, Tibet has been an instrument through which major external protagonists have sought to pursue their wider objectives. Thus, China's interest in Nepal is founded on its own geopolitical security in Tibet. An official at the Lumbini Development Committee confirmed China's active involvement in Lumbini. He (R5) also added that there has been increased presence of pro-Tibet activists in Lumbini in the last couple of years, most of them funded by the United States and other European countries. There are reports of the increasing involvement of China in Nepal not only in the case of Lumbini but also in the politics and development of Nepal (Upadhya, 2016). Such reports go against Indian interests where there is a belief that 'it is in India's interest to see that China does not succeed in its objectives in Nepal . . . and it should not hesitate to use them intelligently to counter the Chinese designs' (Raman, 2011). Foreign media echo the same view. 'China's involvement in a project close to the border with India has caused discomfort in New Delhi, where the government has traditionally regarded itself as a patron of the Buddhist world through its hosting of the Dalai Lama and the Tibetan government in exile' (Dean, 2011 in the *Telegraph*, UK).

It is also important to note that China has assumed a greater role in Nepali tourism lately. The percentage of Chinese visitors has grown significantly in recent years, making China the second-biggest tourism market for Nepal. There is a geopolitical explanation for the growth of the Chinese market. According to Rowen (2016, p. 388), 'China's construction and deployment of Approved Destination Status (ADS) is another example of tourism's political instrumentality'. Since 1995, the Chinese outbound market 'has been regulated by a system that confers ADS on countries that have signed bilateral agreements with China. ADS allows outbound group tourists to apply for visas through travel agencies, saving them a trip to the consulate' (Rowen, 2016, p. 388). Nepal has witnessed constant growth in the number of Chinese tourist arrivals after it was given ADS in 2002.

There are explanations for the geopolitical theories. Acharya (2011) suggests that the APECEF project was Beijing's way of having a 'forward-looking strategy to deal with a post-Dalai Lama Tibet' (Acharya, 2011). According to this view, Lumbini could be pushed as an alternative to Indian plans to revive the ancient heritage sites associated with Lord Buddha. Other respondents took the view that the conflict is over the ownership of Buddhism and its philosophy. They believed that Lumbini's importance in the Buddhist world is very great. For Tibet, this is even more important, because Buddhism forms the core of its culture, and the issue of Tibet goes beyond the freedom of a land, the liberation of a culture, and a celebration of a way of life (Upadhya, 2012).

There is considerable strength in the above argument, as it is well accepted that heritage is knowledge that constitutes both economic and cultural capital (Graham, 2002). Thus, India does not want to lose Lumbini to China, because Buddhism forms an important part of Indian diplomacy with Southeast Asian countries. For example, Ramachandran (2011) writes,

> Although Buddha was born in Nepal, it was in India that all the other important milestones in his life, whether his enlightenment, first sermon or death happened. And it was from India that Buddhism spread to other parts of South, South-East and East Asia. . . . Buddhism forms a core component of India's soft power diplomacy in Asia and it is keen to be a part of the project in Lumbini.

The above statement would appear to be accurate. India sees itself as the 'homeland of Buddhism' (Singh, 2010, p. 194) or a global torchbearer for Buddhism. This is understood as a direct challenge to Nepal's assertion that Lumbini is the birthplace of Buddha. However, given that three out of four places which a pious Buddhist should visit are in India, the above claims by India are not groundless. Additionally, Indian geopolitical interest in Buddhism also emanates from an understanding that the persecution and exile of Tibetan Buddhism has contributed towards revitalising Buddhism in India

(Singh, 2010), and it sees the internationalisation of Tibetan Buddhism as an opportunity that could benefit it in two ways: (a) promoting 'spiritual tourism' in an increasingly globalised world and (b) improving bilateral ties and pan-Buddhist sentiment.

The above factors have led to a distinct and sustained revitalisation of Buddhist pilgrim-cum-tourist circuits in India and also a way to connect with other South Asian nations, with the exception of China. To achieve these objectives, India has been mobilising the regional forums, where it has a dominating influence such as South Asian Association for Regional Cooperation (SAARC) and the Bay of Bengal Initiative for Multi-Sectoral Technical and Economic Cooperation (BIMSTEC). For example, the 18th SAARC declaration, signed by all South Asian leaders, stated, 'they directed to effectively implement the SAARC Agenda for Culture and . . . they also agreed to develop a cultural trail linking major Buddhist historical sites in the region . . .' (MEA, 2016). Similarly, India has been collaborating with the World Bank Group through the International Finance Corporation (IFC) to develop the Buddhist Circuit by attracting higher-spending tourists and linking them to local goods and service providers (World Bank, Undated).

The conquest for the ownership of Buddhism has a strong repercussion for the nationalist sentiment in Nepal because such a claim is easily read as an assertion over Lumbini and an intervention over its autonomy and independence. An important doctrine of nationalists is that the existence of their own nation presupposes the existence of other nations (Triandafyllidou, 1998). In many instances, the 'other' of national communities is often the one from which the community tried to liberate and/or differentiate itself. As Nepal has had more frequent exchange and interactions with India and China throughout its mediaeval history, the conflict between them over Lumbini is bound to raise the alarm by ringing the nationalist tune.

The atmosphere over the Lumbini project has been so charged that the limitations of the geopolitical explanation have hardly received any attention. For example, the geopolitical theory is founded on the argument that the Chinese project is a bogus plan to enter 'the region' because there is no place for religion in China. Even Indian commentators refute such allegations and agree that China is keen to project a Buddhist-friendly image of itself, not only in Tibet but also in other Asian countries (Ramachandran, 2011). Ramachandran (2011) reports that China has renovated scores of Buddhist shrines destroyed during the Cultural Revolution and is involved in the revival of the Nalanda project in India. India is planning to revive the ancient Nalanda civilisation and develop Bodh Gaya as a Buddhist hub. Scholars agree that a confluence of factors such as changing geopolitical contexts and the state's embrace of globalisation can bring two states together (Theva and Mukherji, 2015). There are numerous global forums such as BRICS in which India and China are working together.

Similarly, the geopolitical explanation presumes that China's and India's increasing international clout could contribute to regional conflict. Scholars believe that this is an overestimate (Malone and Mukherjee, 2010). According to Malone and Mukherjee (2010), although China has essentially achieved great-power status, its foreign policy is oriented towards maintaining regional stability and creating conditions for China's 'peaceful rise'. Analysts have characterised China's new diplomacy as 'less confrontational, more sophisticated, more confident, and, at times, more constructive' in its approach to regional and international affairs than it has been in the past (Medeiros and Fravel, 2003). Unlike India's, modern Chinese nationalism is 'pragmatic': it is instrumental and reactive, preoccupied with holding the nation together, in part through a strategy of rapidly accelerating growth rather than with hostility to others.

Ideological differences between the two civilisations

One of the key arguments lost in the above debate was the value-laden worldview on religious heritage and approaches to its development in tourism. There is a scholarly debate that the mobilisation of religious heritage for tourism could be sensitive and needs a more careful examination, because the presence of tourists at a holy place can result in an unbalanced relationship and negative tourism impacts which can burden the host religious community (Joseph and Kavoori, 2001). Such arguments have originated from general concerns that decorum, safety, and security at religious places can be compromised by the presence of tourists (Raj and Morpeth, 2007; Shackley, 2006). As a result, scholars have suggested additional measures to confront them: for instance, Singh (2005) proposes a strict code of conduct for tourists; Nolan and Nolan (1992) suggest scheduling pilgrimage events during a time of year when few tourists visit. Other scholars have suggested charging admission fees, controlling tourist flow, and having restricted zones reserved for pilgrims to separate them from tourists (Garrod, Fyall and Leask, 2006). These concerns point to the fact that tourism is perceived as an activity against which the religious sites need to be protected.

However, it would be helpful to look into a deeper articulation of the role of religion in India and China. Anthropologist van der Veer (2009) argues that the relation between religion and secularism in both countries is a key to understanding similarities and differences between them. According to him, the extent to which religion became central to anti-colonial nationalism in 19th-century India is strikingly important in understanding the country. More recently, the rise of the Bharatiya Janata Party, a Hindu nationalist party, and religious nationalism in general have made the question of religion and its relation to secularism and the secular state central in debates about the future of India. By contrast, in China anti-imperialist nationalism focused on the removal of religion as an obstacle to national progress. The Chinese tend to believe in all sorts of supernatural powers which can intervene in their daily life (Faure, 2000, p. 190); however, their association with religion is not very evident. According to Faure and Fang (2008), during the Cultural Revolution the spiritual dimension of Chinese life was totally banned and replaced by Communist ideology. The theme of religion as 'the opium of the people' was developed to extremes and resulted in the destruction of religious beliefs. As a result, concerns over the spiritual importance of religious sites do not achieve the same level of importance in China as they do in India and Nepal. In China, Buddhist sites have been used for fostering goodwill, either economic or political in nature (Wong, McIntosh and Ryan, 2013). Many religious and sacred sites in China are promoted as historical and cultural sites worth visiting for secular reasons in addition to their religious charisma. Zhang et al. (2007) note that monasteries and temples in China are not necessarily perceived by Han Chinese as holy but often simply as interesting destinations that are worth a visit and provide a 'sense of cultural depth'. Ryan and Gu (2010) look critically at how Buddhism is used politically to create the image of a harmonious society and how the Wu-Tai festival became has become commoditised. Similarly, Zhao (2009) reports how the Shao-Lin Monastery, renowned as the place of origin of Chinese kung-fu, has become a magnet for tourists, to the extent that very few of them even know about its religious significance as the birthplace of Chinese Chan Buddhism founded by Bodhidharma 1,500 years ago.

On the contrary, the case of Hindu religious sites in Nepal and India is different. Nepal forbids non-Hindus from entering its most revered Hindu temple of Pashupatinath, also regarded as a national deity. Similarly, the most holy Hindu religious shrines in India are not open to other faiths. The conservative approach to Hindu religious sites in Nepal and India can be attributed to the strong role of Hindu religion in the two countries. Studies have shown that religious people, across a variety of contexts, tend to attribute high importance to conservative values and low importance to hedonistic and 'openness to change' values (Saroglou, Delpierre and Dernelle, 2004). This has led to disagreement about the development aspects of the project. Scholars have looked into dimensions that indicate how major cultural differences may influence the social relations between international culturally different groups (see Hofstede, 2001; Hofstede and Bond, 1988). The above case also reaffirms the point that cultural groups can differ in many elements that include their approach to social life and human relationships and the perceptions they may develop of others.

Another missed opportunity in this case was that no place was given to other voices in the debate. It was indicated that it would not be prudent to invalidate the claim that the project could be a genuine attempt to develop Lumbini as a heritage tourism hub. A government participant said, 'from whatever I have heard and read the project components are in line with the master plan except for the world's tallest Buddha statue proposed inside the 4 km of the heritage site'. This participant felt that Nepal could benefit from the project. An official at the Lumbini Development Trust also viewed that overall there is nothing wrong with the project, though he has some doubts about whether the APECEF is a bogus organisation, as it has been six years since the APECEF first showed interest in Lumbini, but it has done nothing concrete for its development.

The lack of any serious dialogue around the project in the media was indicative of the literature elsewhere, where the media were used intentionally to generate public sentiment that advances a particular agenda: in effect, propaganda. According to Dittmer (2010, p. xvi), 'the difference between "propaganda" and "truth" often depends on where you stand, and perhaps on the intentions of the producer . . .' which is difficult to assess in the Lumbini case. However, some media seem to advance the geopolitical hypothesis to achieve the propagandist intent 'to obtain the international and internal consensus necessary for the action' (Jean, 1993 cited in Brighi and Petito, 2011, p. 829). As such, they were largely successful in this and, owing to the huge controversy and opposition to the project in the media, the project was shelved for good.

Conclusion

In this chapter, I have looked into the role of Lumbini in the creation and expression of Nepali nationalism through two mediums: (a) through the visit to the heritage site and its visitors, who perceive it as an important element of Nepali national identity, and (b) through the case of an international conflict that has provided a pivotal role in the expression of Nepali national identity. This chapter has also suggested that the conflict at the Lumbini project is the outcome of both internal and external complexities, underpinned by a mix of factors which includes geopolitics and nationalism, interestingly overlooking the factor of the ideological disparity over the understanding of the religious heritage in the two civilisations. The chapter's main propositions are that the Buddha's dominance extends beyond Buddhism in Nepal, and he is an important icon of Nepali national identity; secondly, whether or not geopolitics was its intention, the proposed project has significantly established the perception that Indian and Chinese rivalry has come to Lumbini, as the project was seen as an attempt to encroach upon

Nepali autonomy and nationalism and was strongly opposed. In doing so, the third element, that Chinese understanding of heritage is more utilitarian in contrast to the spiritual value accorded to heritage in Nepal, suggesting that there is a discrepancy in how heritage of that magnitude should be developed, is hardly given any consideration.

The case of Lumbini shows that many important monuments and sites constitute repositories of national identity that make the site a resource for the articulation of national imagination. In the minds of citizens, this makes the site more important than its physical being. For the visitors to Lumbini, it is not important if the Buddha was actually born there, but the current interpretation of the site and the ideology it represents to them is more significant. The recognition of heritage as a monument of global importance has elevated the importance of the place to domestic travellers as well; however, international interest in the Lumbini heritage is also seen as a claim to the ownership of the heritage and a threat to national autonomy, and hence the proposed tourism development project was vigorously opposed. The strong nationalist sentiment attached to the project suggested that public deliberation, that transforms social and political conflicts into argumentative debates, as suggested by Wessler and Schultz (2007), was lacking in Nepal. This gave no opportunity for meaningful articulation of the project or for making claims or counterclaims to arrive at a resolution.

This chapter has also shown that for Nepali visitors, travel to the Lumbini heritage provides a strong sentiment of national feeling and belongingness. Visitors' interpretation of Lumbini and their interaction with the Lumbini heritage evoked a strong self-reflection on their identity and the place of Lumbini in their selfhood. The visit provided an opportunity for them to reassert their belonging to the Nepali nation, and at the same time it also caused them to see themselves vis-à-vis 'the Other'.

In the next chapter I will see how Nepalis living in other countries associate themselves with Nepal during and after their visit home. The purpose of this is to see how travel to Nepal inaugurates a sense of belonging and affinity with the Nepali nation and helps in the articulation of their Nepali nationality and nationhood.

References

Acharya, A. (2011). Lumbini as Geopolitical Ping Pong. *Nepali Times*. Available at: http://nepalitimes.com/news.php?id=18468#.WAh4UySNPZY (accessed 11 January 2012).

Aitchison, C. (1999). Heritage and Nationalism: Gender and the Performance of Power. In D. Crouch (Ed.), *Leisure/Tourism Geographies* (pp. 59–73). London: Routledge.

Anmol, A. (2018). Lumbini Saw More Than 1.55m Tourists in 2017. *The Kathmandu Post*. Available at: http://kathmandupost.ekantipur.com/news/2018-01-13/lumbini-saw-more-than-155m-tourists-in-2017.html.

Ashworth, G. J. (1997). Is There as World Heritage? *Urban Age*, 4(4), 12.

Berger, M. T. (2006). From Nation-Building to State-Building: The Geopolitics of Development, the Nation-State System and the Changing Global Order. *Third World Quarterly*, 27(1), 5–25. DOI: 10.1080/01436590500368719.

Bessière, J. (1998). Local Development and Heritage: Traditional Food and Cuisine as Tourist Attractions in Rural Areas. *Sociologia Ruralis*, 38(1), 21–34.

Bhandari, K. (2016). Understanding Nepali Nationalism. *Studies in Ethnicity and Nationalism*, 16(3), 416–436.

Bidari, B. (2004). *Lumbini: A Haven of Sacred Refuge*. Kathmandu: Hill Side Press (P) Ltd.

Brighi, E. and Petito, F. (2011). The Renaissance of Geopolitics in Post-1989 Italy. *Geopolitics*, 16(4), 819–845. DOI: 10.1080/14650045.2010.548425.

Chaudhary, S. K. (2011). Hiduising Buddhism. *Frontier*, 44(6), August 21–27.

Dean, N. (2011). *Nepal to Build £1.9 Billion 'Buddhist Mecca'*. Available at: www.telegraph.co.uk/news/worldnews/asia/nepal/8582941/Nepal-to-build-1.9-billion-Buddhist-Mecca.html.

Dittmer, J. (2010). *Popular Culture, Geopolitics, and Identity*. Plymouth: Rowman & Littlefield Publishers.

Dixit, K. M. (2011). Between Sycophancy & Adventurism: II. *Republica Daily*, July 28.

Dodds, K. (2005). *Global Geopolitics: A Critical Introduction*. London: Pearson and Prentice Hall.

The Economist. (2011). Available at: www.economist.com/node/21526389.

Faure, G. O. (2000). Traditional Conflict Management in Africa and China. In I. W. Zartman (Ed.), *Traditional Cures for Modern Conflicts: African Conflict Medicine* (pp. 153–165). Boulder, CO: Lynne Rienner Publishers.

Faure, G. O. and Fang, F. (2008). Changing Chinese Values: Keeping Up with Paradoxes. *International Business Review*, 17, 194–207.

Franklin, A. (2003). *Tourism: An Introduction*. London: Sage Publications.

Fuller, G. and Arguilla, J. (1996). The Intractable Problems of Regional Powers. *Orbis*, 40(4), 609–621.

Gaige, F. H. (1975). *Regionalism and National Unity in Nepal*. New Delhi: Vikas Publishing House.

Garrod, B., Fyall, A. and Leask, A. (2006). Managing Visitor Impacts at Visitor Attractions: An International Assessment. *Current Issues in Tourism*, 9(2), 125–151.

Gellner, D. (2016). *The Idea of Nepal*. Kathmandu: Himal Books.

Graham, B. (2002). Heritage as Knowledge: Capital or Culture. *Urban Studies*, 39(5–6), 1003–1017.

Graham, B., Ashworth, G. J. and Tunbridge, J. E. (2000). *A Geography of Heritage: Power, Culture and Economy*. London: Arnold.

Hall, C. M. and Jenkins, J. M. (1995). *Tourism and Public Policy*. London: Routledge.

Hofstede, G. (2001). *Culture's Consequences*. Thousand Oaks, CA: Sage Publications.

Hofstede, G. and Bond, M. (1988). The Confucius Connection: From Cultural Roots to Economic Growth. *Organizational Dynamics*, 16(4), 5–21.

Jean, C. (1993). Voce 'Geopolitica'. In *Enciclopedia delle Scienze Sociali* (Vol. 2). Roma: Istitutodell'Enciclopedia Italiana.

Joseph, C. A. and Kavoori, A. P. (2001). Mediated Resistance: Tourism and the Host Community. *Annals of Tourism Research*, 28(4), 998–1009.

Kraxberger, B. M. and McClaughry, P. A. (2013). South Africa in Africa: A Geo-Political Perspective. *Canadian Journal of African Studies/La Revue canadienne desétudes africaines*, 47(1), 9–25. DOI: 10.1080/00083968.2013.778063.

Lanfant, M. F. (1995). Introduction. In M. F. Lanfant, J. B. Allcock and E. M. Bruner (Eds.), *International Tourism: Identity and Change* (pp. 1–23). London: Sage Publications.

Lowenthal, D. (1998). *The Heritage Crusade and the Spoils of History*. Cambridge: Cambridge University Press.

Malik, M. (2004). India-China Relations: Giants Stir, Cooperate and Compete. *Special Assessment (Asia-Pacific Center for Security Studies)*, October, 1–8. Available at: http://apcss.org/Publications/SAS/AsiaBilateralRelations/India-China RelationsMalik.pdf (accessed 20 December 2011).

Malone, D. M. and Mukherjee, R. (2010). India and China: Conflict and Cooperation. *Survival*, 52(1), 137–158. DOI: 10.1080/00396331003612513.

MEA. (2016). *India-Nepal Joint Statement during the State Visit of Prime Minister of Nepal to India*. Available at: www.mea.gov.in/bilateral-documents.htm? dtl/27407/IndiaNepal_Joint_Statement_during_the_State_visit_of_Prime_ Minister_of_Nepal_to_India.

Medeiros, E. S. and Fravel, M. T. (2003). China's New Diplomacy. *Foreign Affairs*, 82(6), November–December, 22–35. Available at: www.foreignaffairs.com/ articles/asia/2003-11-01/chinas-new-diplomacy (accessed 22 October 2011).

Meskell, L., Liuzza, C., Bertacchini, E. and Saccone, D. (2015). Multilateralism and UNESCO World Heritage: Decision-Making, States Parties and Political Processes. *International Journal of Heritage Studies*, 5, 423–440.

Ministry of Culture, Tourism and Civil Aviation (MoTCA). (2016). *Nepal Tourism Statistics (2016)*. Kathmandu: Government of Nepal.

Naef, P. and Ploner, J. (2016). Tourism, Conflict and Contested Heritage in Former Yugoslavia. *Journal of Tourism and Cultural Change*, 14(3), 181–188.

Nolan, M. L. and Nolan, S. (1992). Religious Sites as Tourism Attractions in Europe. *Annals of Tourism Research*, 19(1), 68–78.

Nyaupane, G. P. (2009). Heritage Complexity and Tourism: The Case of Lumbini, Nepal. *Journal of Heritage Tourism*, 4(2), 157–172. DOI: 10.1080/1743873 0802429181.

Palmer, C. (1999). Tourism and the Symbols of Identity. *Tourism Management*, 20(3), 313–321.

Park, H. (2010). Heritage Tourism: Emotional Journeys to Nationhood. *Annals of Tourism Research*, 37(1), 116–135.

Park, H. (2011). Shared National Memory as Intangible Heritage: Remaining Two Koreans as One Nation. *Annals of Tourism Research*, 38(2), 520–539.

Raj, R. and Morpeth, N. D. (2007). Introduction: Establishing Linkages between Religious Travel and Tourism. In R. Raj and N. D. Morpeth (Eds.), *Religious Tourism and Pilgrimage Management: An International Perspective* (pp. 1–14). Cambridge, USA: CAB International.

Ramachandran, S. (2011). Buddha's Birthplace Courts Controversy. *Asia Times Online.* Available at: www.atimes.com/atimes/South_Asia/MK17Df01.html.

Raman, B. (2011). *Countering China.* Available at: www.outlookindia.com/website/story/countering-china/277608 (accessed 20 November 2012).

Reeves, J. (2012). China's Self-Defeating Tactics in Nepal. *Contemporary South Asia,* 20(4), 525–531.

Republica. (2017). *What Does Dalai Lama Say about Buddha's Birthplace?* Available at: https://myrepublica.nagariknetwork.com/news/what-does-dalai-lama-say-about-buddhas-birthplace/.

Reuters. (2009). Nepal Bans 'Chandni Chowk to China' over Buddha Birth Claim. Available at: http://in.reuters.com/article/idINIndia-37599320090122.

Robinson, M. and Smith, M. (2006). Politics, Power and Play: The Shifting Contexts of Cultural Tourism. In M. Smith and M. Robinson (Eds.), *Cultural Tourism in a Changing World: Politics, Participation and (Re)presentation* (pp. 1–18). Clevedon: Channel View Publications.

Rowen, I. (2016). The Geopolitics of Tourism: Mobilities, Territory and Protest in China, Taiwan, and Hong Kong. *Annals of American Association of Geographers,* 106(2), 385–393.

Ryan, C. and Gu, H. (2010). Constructionism and Culture in Research: Understanding of the Fourth Buddhist Festival, Wutaishan, China. *Tourism Management,* 31(2), 167–178.

Saroglou, V., Delpierre, V. and Dernelle, R. (2004). Values and Religiosity: A Meta-Analysis of Studies Using Schwartz's Model. *Personality and Individual Differences,* 37, 721–734.

Schouten, F. F. J. (1995). Heritage as Historical Reality. In D. T. Herbert (Ed.), *Heritage, Tourism and Society* (pp. 21–31). London: Pinter.

Scott, D. (2008). The Great Power 'Great Game' between India and China: 'The Logic of Geography'. *Geopolitics,* 13(1), 1–26. DOI: 10.1080/14650040701783243.

Shackley, M. (2006). Empty Bottles at Sacred Sites: Religious Retailing at Ireland's National Shrine. In D. J. Timothy and D. H. Olsen (Eds.), *Tourism, Religion and Spiritual Journeys* (pp. 94–103). London and New York: Routledge.

Singh, S. (2005). Secular Pilgrimages and Sacred Tourism in the Indian Himalayas. *GeoJournal,* 64(3), 215–223.

Singh, U. (2010). Exile and Return: The Reinvention of Buddhism and Buddhist Sites in Modern India. *South Asian Studies,* 26(2), 193–217. DOI: 10.1080/02666030.2010.514744.

Smith, L. (2006). *Uses of Heritage.* London: Routledge.

Tewari, R. C. (1983). Socio-Cultural Aspects of Theravada Buddhism in Nepal. *The Journal of the International Association of Buddhist Studies,* 6(2), 67–93.

Theva, Y. S. O. and Mukherji, R. (2015). India-Singapore Bilateral Relations (1965–2012): The Role of Geo-Politics, Ideas, Interests, and Political Will. *India Review,* 14(4), 419–439. DOI: 10.1080/14736489.2015.1092745.

THT. (2016). Available at: www.hindustantimes.com/india-news/tibet-infrastructure-gives-beijing-edge-over-india-in-nepal-chinese-media/story-Q1RgxZ9l8tNrc PMJVLNimK.html (accessed 28 October 2016).

Times of India (TOI). (2009). *Ramesh Sippy Expresses Regret over CC2C Row in Nepal.* Available at: http://articles.timesofindia.indiatimes.com/2009-01-23/south-asia/28009216_1_maoist-government-upendra-yadav-lumbini.

Triandafyllidou, A. (1998). National Identity and the 'Other'. *Ethnic and Racial Studies,* 21(4), 593–612.

Tucker, H. and Carnegie, E. (2014). World Heritage and the Contradictions of 'Universal Value'. *Annals of Tourism Research,* 47, 63–76.

Upadhya, S. (2012). *Nepal and the Geostrategic Rivalry between China and India.* London: Routledge.

van der Veer, P. (2009). The Comparative Sociology of India and China. *Social Anthropology,* 17(10), 90–108.

Wessler, H. and Schultz, T. (2007). Can the Mass Media Deliberate? Insight from Print Media and Political Talk Shows. In R. Butsch (Ed.), *Media and Public Spheres.* London: Palgrave Macmillan.

West II, W. J. (2006). Religion as Dissident Geopolitics? Geopolitical Discussions within the Recent Publications of Fethullah Gülen. *Geopolitics,* 11(2), 280–299. DOI: 10.1080/14650040600598536.

Wong, W. U. I., McIntosh, A. and Ryan, C. (2013). Buddhism and Tourism: Perceptions of Monastic Community at Pu-Tuo-Shan, China. *Annals of Tourism Research,* 40, 213–234.

World Bank. (Undated). *Investing in the Buddhist Circuit (2014–2018): Enhancing the Spiritual, Environmental, Social and Economic Value of the Places Visited by the Buddha in Bihar and Uttar Pradesh, India.* New Delhi: International Finance Corporation the World Bank Group.

Zhang, M., Huang, L., Wang, J. H., Liu, J., Jie, Y. G. and Lai, X. T. (2007). Religious Tourism and Cultural Pilgrimage: A Chinese Perspective. In R. Raj and N. D. Morpeth (Eds.), *Religious Tourism and Pilgrimage Management: International Perspective* (pp. 98–112). Cambridge, MA: CAB International.

Zhao, D. (2009). Transformation of the Sacred: The Commercialization, Politicization and Globalization of Buddhist Heritage Tourism in China Today. Paper presented at the International Conference on *Heritage in Asia: Converging Forces and Conflicting Values.*

5 Earthquake and diasporic travel to homeland

Introduction

On the 25th of April 2015, Nepal was struck by an earthquake of a magnitude of 7.8 that killed more than 8,800 people and injured another 23,000. It displaced hundreds of thousands of people and made them homeless, and many villages were flattened in the affected regions (National Planning Commission, 2015). The earthquake was a huge blow to the country that was recovering from a decade-long civil war and political turmoil. Tourism was the worst-hit sector, as the earthquake occurred during the first of the two major tourism seasons of the year. According to the Post Disaster Needs Assessment report prepared by the Government of Nepal, nine out of ten planned foreign arrivals cancelled in the aftermath of the quake. Seven out of 10 World Heritage sites in the Kathmandu Valley were directly affected, including some popular trekking routes. In terms of heritage, the earthquake affected about 2,900 structures with a cultural, historical, and religious heritage value. Major monuments in Kathmandu's World Heritage Monument Zones were severely damaged, and many were completely destroyed. In addition, in more than 20 districts, thousands of private residences built on traditional lines, historic public buildings and ancient and recently built temples and monasteries were destroyed by the disaster. The Post Disaster Needs Assessment prepared by the Government of Nepal suggested the total estimated damage to tangible heritage was around US$ 169 million.

The aftermath of the earthquake witnessed a remarkable engagement of the Nepali diasporic community throughout the world in the relief and rebuilding process. To the diasporic communities, the earthquake provided a setting for the expression of feelings and love for their home country. As a result, a considerable number of Nepalis from all around the world visited 'home'. Those who could not visit their families sent back money: for example, a study by the Asia Foundation found that there was an increase in remittances from some countries in the weeks following the earthquake (The Asia Foundation, 2015). Many diasporic organisations helped raise money through charities, and some of them sent contingents of volunteers to directly engage with rescue and relief operations in Nepal. For example, the Non-Resident Nepalese Association mobilised its chapters across the world to raise money and sent their volunteers to help in the relief and rescue operations. Many other emigrant Nepalis acted in their individual capacity. The earthquake instilled a sense of loss and provided an opportunity to bring people from all around the world to connect with their home nation.

This chapter examines how diasporic visitors recollect 'home' during and after their visit and how such recollections contribute to their homeland identity and sense of belonging to their home nation. The chapter is based on the narratives of the Nepali diasporic community in the UK who visited Nepal following the devastating earthquake in April 2015. It demonstrates that for those communities, the notions of 'home' and personal memory play an important part in negotiating the bonding with and the sense of belonging to the Nepali nation, enabling them to reconnect with their country of origin. I argue that the articulation of root, identity, and belongingness and the expression of feelings and show of love for the country in the context of Nepali diasporic communities is an expression of nationalism.

Memory, diaspora, tourism, and nationalism

This chapter is based on the notion that diasporic memories and performances act as a repository of diasporic consciousness. The earthquake provided a context for the Nepali diaspora to revisit their 'memories' of the 'home' nation and inspired people to visit the country in the immediate aftermath. The April earthquake is a landmark event in the history of the Nepali nation that every member of the diaspora, irrespective of whether they were in the home nation at the time, can presumably recollect, share, and identify with and has become an important reference point in the expression of group identity. Urry (1996) argues that memory is social in nature, that is, people remember together. Some scholars take the view that as a form of awareness, memory is wholly and intensely personal; it is always felt as 'some particular event (that) happened to me' (Lowenthal, 1995, p. 194). Nevertheless, every recollection, however personal it may be, even that of events of which we alone were the witnesses, even that of thoughts and sentiments that remain unexpressed, exists in relationship with a whole ensemble of notions which many others possess (Connerton, 1989, p. 36). Such sharing of recollections is important because through them we recover consciousness of former events. For the diasporic community, this is even more important, because the remembering of the past is crucial for their sense of identity; recalling past experiences links us with our earlier selves, however different they may since have become (Urry, 1996). Thus, the intent of this chapter is to look into the recollections of diasporic visits to 'home nation' after Nepal's devastating earthquake and to see how they contribute to the traveller's homeland memory and how it emboldens their homeland nationalism.

The concept of home and homeland can be varied in scope and meaning. One strand of research on 'home' posits it as a fixed and bounded place that plays an important role in grounding people to a particular place (Ralph and Staeheli, 2011). Another approach treats 'home' as a mobile concept where the idea extends and connects people and places across time and space (Datta, 2010; Brettell, 2006); this is very relevant for the present study on migrants. The speed, intensity, frequency, and volume of human mobility and migration have so much changed the world that both place of origin and destination influence migrants' routine practices and everyday lives (Urry, 2000; Al-Ali and Khoser, 2002; Baldassar, 1997). According to this view, home is built through a dynamic process of localising particular sets of relationships that do not necessarily depend on the essential qualities of a particular geographical place (Nowicka, 2007). Thus, home is a process involving both the people we share 'home' with and the material objects therein (Ralph and Staeheli, 2011, p. 519).

The above idea of 'home' is inextricably linked with the notion of belongingness, because the same relationships and processes that construct 'home' are also involved in creating identities and feelings of belonging (Ralph and Staeheli, 2011). To belong means to find a place where an individual can feel 'at home', whereby home stands for a symbolic space of familiarity, comfort, security, and emotional attachment (Antonsich, 2010). For diasporic communities, 'home' is a way to express their belongingness which is articulated through their sense of self. Place-based attachments form a key part in this process, as belonging to a place becomes one and the same as belonging to a group of people; belonging becomes synonymous with identity, both social and individual (Brown, 2011; Christou, 2011). Thus, belongingness can be understood as a representational practice of the diasporic condition which provides a strong emotional sense of support and identity (Bess, Fisher, Sonn and Bishop, 2002).

Such feelings of belonging give rise to diasporic tourism: a sense of self-identity and the search for 'ancestry' are among the reasons for people to take return journeys (Wright, 2009). Such journeys can rouse diasporic consciousness, often associated with myths and nostalgia and with imagined and actual histories of the group (Coles and Timothy, 2004, p. 13) and can function as a means to 'renew, reiterate and solidify familial and social networks' (Duval, 2004, p. 51). As there are many reasons for people to travel to their homeland, most studies on diasporic travel are concerned with motivations. Many conclude that diasporic consciousness and long-ing for root identity are the main reasons for 'homeland' travel (Bhandari, 2013; Basu, 2007; Leite, 2005). If we consider that in many cases homeland travel could be triggered not by intrinsic desire or longing for home alone but by external factors, then the question arises whether such travel can still provide room for the articulation of identity and belongingness. Thus, in this chapter, I will first look into the production of 'home' and 'memory' in the daily performances of the Nepali diasporic community and then examine how the sense of home and belongingness is articulated while discussing the earthquake and its influence on their subsequent homeland travel.

Diasporas and other transnational circumstances can play a role in the development of nationalism (Mulligan, 2002). Brubaker (1996) termed this type of nationalism 'homeland nationalism', which is 'directed "outward" across the boundaries of territory and citizenship, towards members of their own ethnic nationality, that is towards persons who "belong" (or can be claimed to belong) to the external national homeland by ethnonational affinity, although they reside in and are (ordinarily) citizens of other states' (p. 111). Other scholars have termed it 'long-distance nationalism' (Ander-son, 1992; Schiller and Fouron, 2002). This long-distance nationalism brings together those who share a sense of 'peoplehood' based on shared culture and history by situating people in their ancestral homeland. Schiller and Fouron (2002) note that an 'increasing number of states are develop-ing legal ways of reclaiming emigrants and their descendants' (p. 357). But distinctively long-distance nationalism cannot be imposed by a state or be seen as 'top down' but springs from the life experiences of migrants whose lives extend across borders.

Many diasporic groups reside and function in a host country but retain strong emotional and allegiance connections to their countries of ori-gin (Kelly, 2000; Sheffer, 1986, cited in Timothy, 2008). This emotional bonding with their homeland opens immense opportunities for gov-ernments back home. China and India have seen unprecedented return investment by their diasporic communities for the economic development of their countries. Diasporic groups can also be useful politically. A good example is Croatia, where the government encouraged visits by diasporic Croatians as a way of garnering support for independence from Yugosla-via, and these tourists were encouraged to play several important political roles (Carter, 2004). Additionally, the Irish case of 'Homecoming' also shows that the promotional drive geared towards diasporas cannot be free from political and cultural agendas (Morgan, Pritchard and Pride, 2002). In terms of various variants of nationalism, the ideas of roots and ancestral belongings are an important basis of ethnic nationalism (Nash, 2002). Smith (1991) typifies nationalism as being of two distinct kinds: territorial or civic and ethnic nationalism. Most commonly the Western version of nationalism is defined as civic and the Eastern version as the ethnic category.

Outmigration in the Nepali context

Separation from home or homeland is relatively new to Nepalis. Though Nepalis have migrated from their ancestral villages to newer pastures, this has been mostly confined within their national border. The very limited external migration that took place in the mediaeval period was largely to India for religious purposes and to Lhasa in Tibet for trading purposes. The more recent form of migration only started in the last quarter of the 20th century, and much of it was for economic reasons. Traditional destinations were India, Hong Kong, Japan, and other areas in the Asiatic mainland. This pattern of migration began to change from the 1990s, when Nepalis opted for Gulf countries such as Kuwait and Qatar. Later on this triggered a movement farther west, since immigration laws in Hong Kong and Japan began to tighten (Gellner, 2013).

Migration to the United States (US) and Europe is fairly new. Earlier migrants to the US belonged to a group that dared to 'dream big', and those who succeeded had certain objectives, notably, to study in an advanced educational environment. People with this desire were and still are facilitated by agencies which provide guidance and counselling back home. Other migrants were attracted by the prospects of work and earning money (Gellner, 2013). Another important factor that has aided increased migration to the US is the Diversity Visa (DV) lottery system. The programme is congressionally mandated and allows up to 55,000 persons from nations that are historically under-represented in terms of migration to the US to qualify each year for immigrant visas. Since Nepal is on the eligibility list, a large number of Nepalis immigrate to the US through this system every year. These immigrants secure their Green Card, become permanent residents, and join the ranks of the 'diaspora' (Gellner, 2013).

The situation differs to some extent in the UK. Migration to that country during the 1970s and 80s related to scholarships offered to Nepali medical doctors and civil servants. The number of Nepalis started to increase after 1997, when Gurkhas, Nepali men serving in the British Army, were allowed to settle in the UK upon retirement (see Gellner, 2013). The trend continued further after May 2009, when the government conceded the right for all ex-Gurkhas with four years of service to settle in the UK. Today, Nepalis are the fastest-growing ethnic minority in the UK (Adhikary, 2012). According to the 2011 UK census, the estimated number of Nepalis in the UK is 60,202, which is a significant rise from the 5,938 recorded in the 2001 census. Even the 2011 census data are considered to be below the actual number, since a study in 2008 already estimated the Nepali population in the UK to be 72,173 (Adhikary, 2012). Though ex-servicemen form a large portion, the Nepali community in the UK is diverse, comprising more than two dozen ethnic groups (see Gellner, 2015).

Gellner (2015) suggests that a Nepali community in the UK cannot be taken as internally homogenous from the point of view of various attributes such as ethnicity, religion, ritual, and so on. This has great implications for the study of the Nepali diaspora. For example, many ethnic groups have their own claim over separate territories as 'homeland'. These groups have discrete ethnic homeland movements in Nepal and have undergone different migratory trajectories. We have noted in Chapter 2 that Barth (1981) takes the view that ethnic groups are categories of ascription and identification by the actors themselves, and the nature and continuity of their self-identity depends on the maintenance of a boundary with the 'Other' or the outsider. In such cases, 'homeland' is not always remembered in the same way, and reference to 'home' or 'homeland' by members of different ethnic groups could significantly vary in meaning because of increased ethnic polarisation in Nepal. This has also been supported by Brusle (2012), who states that diasporas can never be homogenous; the author has shown that the structure of the Nepali diasporic community reflects the tensions of Nepali society. Thus, the various ethnic groups in the UK may be speaking in the name of their 'homeland', but this is understood as a place of their specific ethnic identity and origin.

To accommodate the multiplicity of Nepali communities and their diversity, I will include the 'diasporic stances, claims or practices' (Brubaker, 2005, p. 13) that for each of these constituencies represent 'home'. Brubaker (2005) states that the proliferation of 'diaspora' in the last two decades has expanded the meaning of the term so much that it is scattered in all directions. There is a tendency to conceptualise all emigrant groups as diasporas, including those from Nepal. However, Subba (2008) argues that Indian Nepalis are not diaspora, as most of them were born in India and have no memories of Nepal and no wish to visit Nepal. This cautions us to avoid the fallacy of a blanket approach that treats all overseas Nepali communities as diaspora. Thus, drawing on Brubaker, I take diaspora to mean a category of practice rather than a bounded group. A similar approach is suggested by Hausner and Gellner (2012): their study of 'Nepali religion' has shown that the religious practices of Nepalis in the UK involve a ritualised behaviour that may or may not fit into fixed religious categories as defined by the census.

Tourism and the Nepali diasporic communities

Contrary to many other diasporic communities, Nepalis immigrated to the UK voluntarily, in other words, without a direct act of coercion. They are free to go back to their home country, and the sense of loss is presumably comparatively lower than for certain other groups, such as refugees. Schiller and Fouron (2002, p. 357) note that an 'increasing number of states are developing legal ways of reclaiming emigrants and their descendants', though this is not the case in Nepal. Since the migration itself has happened because of people's desire rather than compulsion, the question of return visits does not appear high on the diasporic agenda. Pariyar, Shrestha, and Gellner (2014), however, report that among the ex-British Gurkha servicemen of the UK, there is some intention to return to Nepal after seeing their children settled here. Even if there is a fair number of people returning, this will hardly find any place in Nepal's tourism strategy, because, according to existing definitions, Nepalis are not considered tourists. Nepal's Tourism Act of 1978 defines tourists as those non-Nepali citizens coming to Nepal for a visit from a foreign country. The association between tourism and diaspora has been geared more towards mobilising diaspora to promote Nepal as a destination for foreign tourists. For example, the Nepal Tourism Board appoints Nepali entrepreneurs based in the host country as its honorary PR representatives. For entrepreneurs this is a privilege, as reflected in a restaurant owner's statement (R1): 'this is the way I am fulfilling my duty towards my motherland'.

The mobilisation of diaspora was attempted in a 'Send Home a Friend' campaign in 2007. This was not intended for Nepalis themselves as tourists, but they were asked to send their friends to visit Nepal. It was a well-thought-out programme at the time when Nepal was battling with a poor image due to internal political instability. The use of the word 'home' was carefully chosen to appeal to the diasporic sentiment and was aimed at garnering support from the vast network of Nepalis scattered around the world. The programme provided free promotional collaterals to the diasporic Nepali community and friends of Nepal. However, the campaign was fully owned by neither the tourism board nor the diasporic communities and was not a success. For example, the influential Trekking Agents Association of Nepal claimed that fewer than 20 visitors came to the country through the campaign in the fiscal year 2007/08 (TAAN, 2009). The campaign was originally conceived by a very senior bureaucrat in the Ministry of Tourism who later headed the Nepali civil service; as a result, it was extended to 2009 and 2010 in the run-up to the 'Nepal Tourism Year' celebration in 2011. During the promotion of Nepal Tourism Year 2011, a television advertisement was prepared in which some youths along with Miss Nepal 2010 were shown discussing their next plan to visit their ancestral home in rural Nepal. But this was intended for domestic consumption and targeted at the population displaced internally due to various socio-economic factors (personal communication with a senior officer in Nepal Tourism Board).

Diasporic travel to the 'nation' after the earthquake

The above paragraphs show how mobility of culture and cultural objects can help create feelings of 'home' and belongingness and how some forms of travel, notably leisure trips to established tourist routes in the home country and gifts that travel from the host to the home destination, can be associated with creating boundaries. How did such construction of boundaries impact the immigrants' feelings and emotions when they travelled to the homeland in the wake of the April earthquake? In the following section, I will show in more detail how the idea of home or belongingness and cognition of boundary or self-identity inform and are embedded in Nepalis' homeland travel in the aftermath of the earthquake. A quote from a Nepali NHS nurse from the UK who visited the country after the earthquake articulates the notion of home and collective identity. She states,

> I was proud to visit Nepal at a time when our nation was needing me. I felt immense satisfaction to serve my countrymen, after all we are one family, belonging to the same home. I see it emboldened by feeling towards my nation and felt this feeling towards your nation brings us all together.

The above quote is important in understanding how the element of collective identity connects Nepali diasporas to their homeland. In the above case, the use of the words 'home' and 'nation' tries to capture that sense of common identity. Billig (2001) has looked into how a nation is daily reminded of nationhood by the use of words, 'we', 'us', 'our': and homeland is imagined as an entity in the sense that 'it is the place of "our" personal homes – my home, your home – and, as such, it is the home of all of "us", the home of the homes, the place where all of "us" are at home' (p. 75). In the view of diasporic visitors, a strong emotional attachment exists between diasporas and their 'native' land. Travel to Nepal in the above case was instrumental to them in their self-identity and cultural affinity.

Similarly, a comment was made by another participant who was in Nepal visiting his home and consoling the family members who were severely hit by the earthquake. He stated,

> This visit has made me aware of my identity and my duty towards my community and fellow countrymen. It helped me realise that we

all have same ethnicity, which is called Nepali. I left for Nepal leaving my family here, however after reaching Kathmandu I realised how mistaken I was. There was a whole nation helping each other as a family. I realised I belonged not to my *Newar* community but to a Nepali ethnicity.

Another participant stated that the visit was instrumental in rethinking who he is. He admitted,

> After I returned from my visit to Nepal, I started to see myself as differently. Though I may reside and work in this country, my root lies in Nepal. Though I may speak English in my workplace here, I have a separate language and culture that has a long history. I then realised how important it is for my children to know one's cultural heritage and practise it.

A close relationship between ethnicity and roots in the study of nations and nationalism means that the yearning for roots and an ethnic past is closely linked to the idea of nativeness. The strong association between home travel and its positive relation to enhanced root identity also resonates with nationalism, because a strong sense of belonging to an 'authentic' nation is the premise of the ideals of nationalism. However, where does this authority of 'travelling to home nation' as a nationalistic force come from? The answer can be found in the fact that travel and tourism has a vast organic role in the making of peoples, in the manufacture of places, and in the manipulation of pasts (Hollinshead, 1998). This organic role of homeland travel in manipulating people, place, and past can be an immense repository in the forming of an organic identity. Smith (1991) makes the point that the awareness of an organic identity is importantly related to the idea of nation:

> A historic land is one where terrain and people have exerted mutual, and beneficial, influence over several generations. The homeland becomes a repository of historic memories and associations, the place where 'our' sages, saints and heroes lived, worked, prayed and fought. All this makes the homeland unique. Its rivers, coasts, lakes, mountains and cities become 'sacred' places of veneration and exaltation whose inner meanings can be fathomed by the initiated, that is, the self-aware members of the nation.
>
> (p. 9)

Many other participants took the similar view that they did not travel to Nepal for a normal visit or celebration but primarily for the purpose of being with fellow countrymen at a time of need. They emphasised that it creates a very different and special feeling, a great deal of self-fulfilment and sense of achievement when you go back to your home on such a mission. They thought that it was a different and difficult trip, but they felt proud of having travelled to Nepal at this historical time. To many of them this visit has made them re-realise their self-identity and where they come from. There was a deep sense of pain and belongingness in the expressions of many people who travelled home. A former tourism entrepreneur, who now lives in the UK, said the following of her love for the country,

> Not only Nepal is grieving at this time, Nepali hearts all over the world have been broken along with the historical and natural heritage that [was] lost in this tragedy [. . .]. We are grieving because we have lost our heritage bequeathed to us by ancestors; we are also grieving because pride and dignity have been shattered. Single Nepal has grieved from the plains of the south to the high Himalayas in the north.

Loss of some of Nepal's iconic monumental and sacred buildings is a huge setback to the nation's heritage, which relies on the notion of memory being bound to a place and captured in an artefact or historic objects, as well as the heritage industry that is of crucial economic importance to Nepal. To the above participant the demolition of such objects and heritage icons implied the destruction of the homeland's 'containers of memory' (Marschall, 2015, p. 336).

Mensah (2015) has shown in the case of the African diaspora visiting Ghana that homeland travel can be an emotional journey in which expressions of grief, sorrow, and loss are extensive. In fact, emotional engagement is the reason for home travel, argues Leite (2005). A participant described the beginning of her journey this way: 'with heart filled with love and eyes with tears, we embarked on our journey to Nepal'. She feels being there is different to hearing about it from others,

> There is a great difference between hearing from others and seeing it, probably facing it yourself would . . . be different. Even now my imaginations are filled with flattened heritage sites and people's grieving pain. I keep [being] reminded of the injured people. The [uncertain] future seen in the eyes of innocent children keeps me waking up.

Returning to the homeland is a journey through memory, moments of cultural (re)discovery, and experiences of longing and belonging (Vathi and King, 2011). According to Marschall (2012a, 2012b), such journeys can involve revisiting one's lost family home, one's old school, the place one used to play as a child, and many other sites where key moments in one's life occurred. The following example testifies to the above view and shows the feelings of a US–based Nepali politician upon seeing the extent of devastation in one of his childhood haunts:

> My heart was filled with tears after seeing the devastation in the Basantapur durbar square where I was brought up, where I played, did my school assignments and spent my childhood. It was lifeless, like a war-torn region. All its history was eclipsed by the devastation.
>
> (Rauniyar, 2015)

Leite (2005) uses the term 'imaginative reconstruction' to describe diasporic yearnings to relive the past. It is through this reconstruction that tourists engage, not merely sensing the past or reliving ancestral experience in the present but actually imagining themselves 'there and then'. The above quote brings the case of such connection. This is also similar to another study of Irish immigrants to the UK by Hughes and Allen (2010), who found that a desire to visit was expressed by some older informants as an opportunity to recapture childhood memories, and in that sense Ireland was interpreted as 'home' – a place of origin. For the above individual the visit also offered a chance to restore his 'childhood through memories' (Vathi and King, 2011). On many occasions travel home arouses 'reflective nostalgia' (Boym, 2001) in which one cherishes fragments of memory, which could be objects, stories, or texts. The devastation created by the earthquake was one such stimulus for the above participant.

While nostalgia is a yearning for the past, a different place and time, possibly our childhood when time appeared to move more slowly (Boym, 2001), visits home can sometimes foster a yearning for a better future as well. This is often seen in the form of nationalistic feelings. Rauniyar (2015) writes, '[t]his is the time to do something for the country, this is the time to wake up the country and take it to prosperity. It is the time to transform the country, time for a new leader to emerge'. Hutt (1998) argues that a diasporic consciousness is more conspicuously present in the literary productions of nationalist intellectuals than it is in the minds, hearts, and actions of working-class cosmopolitans. However, there were many instances in which such expressions were equally common in the opinion of ordinary members of the Nepali diaspora. The following is an example:

> I felt [a] great sense of pride for having this opportunity to touch the hundreds-of-years' old bricks during the rescue in Tripureshwor. I was overwhelmed by my patriotic feelings. This is time to show love for

your motherland – to express your patriotism. It is during the time of pain that you heal your country through your love and care.

In the case of diaspora there is always an element of 'travel down memory lane'. Sheller and Urry (2004) argue that tourism and other types of mobility are part of the same complex and interconnected system, each producing the other. According to them, there is a proliferation of countless discourses, forms, and embodiments of tourist places and tourist performance, and as such, tourism sometimes can be 'unreal'. This reinforces the idea that holidays do not have to involve physical travel; we can move between different modes of doing; being a tourist is not necessarily place or time specific (Larsen, 2008; Gale, 2009). Some expressions evoke this element of mobility, where travel is still continuing in the mind even after the completion of the physical journey. A participant expressed it this way,

> Though my body is in the US, my heart is always loitering in Nepal. Let alone the patriotic Nepalis, anyone would not be untouched by the suffering of the Nepali citizens at this time.
>
> (Siwakoti, 2015, English translation by author)

The above example illustrates well that a cultural sense of belonging is often maintained by bringing back visual reminders and memories, as argued by Vathi and King (2011). The case of the Nepali diaspora shows that it can also be brought back with the element of 'experience' retained in the form of memory. A similar example is seen in the following expression:

> The suffering the country is facing has put every Nepali living abroad in pain. It does not matter where one lives physically, but it is the heart which is greater than this. My body is in the UK but my soul is still wandering in Nepal all the time.

Identifying with the polity of the 'home nation'

In usual parlance, 'diaspora' suggests a dislocation from the original nation-state or geographical location (Braziel and Mannur, 2003). However, in the case of the Nepali diaspora, they are very well connected with their home nation. They closely follow everyday affairs in Nepal and keep abreast with latest developments through various news media and online portals. Many diasporic communities and groups maintain a keen interest in the activities of political parties and the working of the government in Nepal. All participants expressed their deep sadness about the political instability in Nepal and its implications for the post-earthquake reconstruction in Nepal. It is useful to note that following the April earthquake, the government of Nepal established a National Reconstruction Authority (NRA) in Parliament in December 2015. The main task of the Authority was to ease the procedures for the distribution of grants, relocation of settlements deemed at risk, and the distribution of vital construction materials. However, the organisation has been mired in political instability, and every change in government has changed the leadership of the NRA. At the time of writing this book, the Authority was set to witness a change in its CEO for the fifth time in the last three years.

Members of the Nepali diaspora community were fully apprised of the political developments in the 'home' country and its impact on the government's reconstruction work. For example, a participant said,

It is deeply saddening to see the political mismanagement adding to the plight of my countrymen affected by the earthquake. I am utterly displeased by the response of the Nepali state and its failure in mobilising its agencies in the reconstruction work. Our dear brothers and sisters had to languish in makeshift tents for months because of political wrangling over the creation and mandate over the NRA. When finally they did form the NRA it has not worked very satisfactorily. I think the behaviour of top politicians has been very selfish and insensitive towards the plight of the common Nepalis affected by the earthquake.

The above comments remind us of the earlier remarks that not all diasporas are identical. Scholars have maintained that every diaspora is different, and they reflect the specificities of their conditions, histories, new homeland immigration policies, and population sizes (Timothy and Coles, 2004). In Nepal, people's affiliation with political parties and their familiarity with the political affairs is very common. It is the same with the Nepali diasporic community members, most of whom are affiliated with one or other political or ethnic groups in Nepal, suggesting that the people in the diaspora do exhibit 'home' characteristics in their new nation.

Another point is that diasporas keep connected with their homeland through various channels. For example, Harper (2003) has analysed two main means of contact that Scottish migrants make to stay in touch with their original homeland and preserve their Scottish identities. They are formal mechanisms such as 'church, school and Scottish society' and informal mechanisms such as 'place names, correspondence, family and community networks and chain migration' (p. 370). According to Gellner (2013), Nepali case shows that shows that they maintain their contact with Nepal through their association with community groups or place-based groups.

Most people in this study confirmed that they are members of their respective groups such as Gulmi Samaj or Tamu Samaj UK.

In some instances, participants used their memories of earlier earthquakes to connect with the state and government of the home country. They used their personal experience and knowledge of the country to make connections with the state. For example, a participant said,

> I think earthquakes are not new to our country (Nepal). In 1988 when the earthquake struck in the very early hours of the morning, I was fast asleep in my maternal uncle's home in *Dharan*. We all quickly came out of the house and took shelter on the large playing field beside the road. People were treated in the temporary health camps and in the local government hospital. I remember there were police and army personnel helping in the rescue and reconstruction. We received government assistance for the re-building of our partly damaged house in Dhankuta.

The above case points to the important factor of the individual's identifying with the nation. Cohen (1996) assigns the primacy of their selfhood and self-identity as 'personal nationalism'. According to him, one can see the nation by looking at oneself. He argues that by looking at oneself or one's experience, one's reading of history, perception of the landscape, and reading of literature and music, one can see the nation. It is on sharing personal experiences that sentiment and attachment to the nation is predicated. The above quotes remind us that people's association and identification with the nation is determined and dictated by their personal life experience.

Additionally, the above reference of their own experience of earthquake can be explained through the idea of existential authenticity. Wang (1999) characterises the ideal of authenticity by either nostalgia or romanticism. It is nostalgic because it idealises the ways of life in which people are supposed to be freer, more innocent, more spontaneous, purer, and truer to themselves than usual – such ways of life are usually supposed to exist in the past or in childhood. It is also romantic because it accents the naturalness, sentiments, and feelings in response to the increasing self-constraints of reason and rationality in modernity. The participant's mention of his encounter with earthquake during his childhood can be interpreted as an attempt towards search of their authentic selves, in which memory plays a role.

Interestingly, it also appeared that interaction with the various institutions of the nation provides a useful insight in the way belongingness with the nation is expressed. Some of the interviewees expressed their unhappiness and displeasure with the changes in the Nepali constitution and in particular the constitutional change that has made Nepal a secular federal republic. They related with the earlier regime and used this to claim ownership of the nation. They also tried to demonise the identity enshrined in the new constitution by using the earthquake as a case of divine intervention, rejecting the new provision. For example, a participant said,

> In my opinion, Nepal and the Himalayas is an abode for Hindu gods and goddesses. I believe the earthquake is the medium through which God has expressed his dissatisfaction over the recent changes made in the constitution.

Another participant compared the situation with the earlier regime and said,

> During the times of our childhood we were safe and never had to deal with such disasters. There was no need for such disasters because the country was ruled by the King. Now our countrymen have to live in constant fear of earthquakes or other such disasters. More of them are happening now than before. This is because they have removed the 'protector' of the country (i.e., the King) from his rightful place.

The above comments highlight how people take refuge in the idea of fatalism to connect with the nation imagined by them. In his seminal book *Fatalism and Development*, Bista (1999) has discussed the fatalist character of Nepali society. Fatalism refers to a belief 'that has no personal control over one's life circumstances, which are determined through a divine or powerful external agency' (1999, p. 5). According to Bista, this fatalistic resignation was exploited by a powerful minority group consisting of high-caste Hindus and others until the 1990s to strengthen the king's position in Nepali society. Though fatalistic sentiment has received a strong challenge in recent years after the various ethnic and indigenous groups were allowed freedom to express themselves, the idea is still strong amongst diasporic members belonging to certain religious orientations and caste groups. Additionally, there is still a significant section of diasporic groups who adhere to the belief that the king should still lead the country, and the above comment reflects such a viewpoint. However, the above examples strengthen the point that there is multiplicity in the way people interact with their nation and which strongly defines how they imagine their home 'nation'.

Conclusions

In this chapter, I have discussed how the Nepali diaspora's travel to their native land reconnects them with their root identity. The importance of diasporas comes from the fact that the 'true nation' was imagined as a 'moral community' being formed centrally by the 'natives' in exile (Malkki,

1992): travel to one's roots and heritage gives a sense of belongingness and reconnection with their root identity and realises their authentic self. This realisation has the propensity to reinforce one's cultural identity and helps create solidarity with their ancestral homeland and its people. This happens because of common ancestry and is an expression of nationalism, as it is associated with 'a consciousness of belonging to the nation, its sentiments and aspirations' (Smith, 1991, p. 72).

The case of the Nepali diaspora also suggests their strong connection with developments in Nepal. The dissatisfaction over the failure of the state to deliver to people affected by the earthquake was a strong testimony to this. The language in their narrative and very frequent use of collective nouns like 'we' or 'our' while making reference to Nepal or Nepali is an interesting indication of their strong sense of belonging to Nepal. These references to Nepal and its institutions indicates that their sense of belongingness is not limited to them as part of the Nepali cultural world, but it is evidence of how they feel these institutions are part of their identity as well. The case of the diaspora also shows how they are using memory to advance the version of identity they are familiar with and which they feel is appropriate. The reference to an earlier form of Nepali national identity that relied on monarchy and the Hindu religion as a strong form of identification is interesting and shows how some diaspora are finding it difficult to connect with the aspirations of present-day Nepal. The chapter also suggests that Nepali identity cannot be understood as fixed, but it is constantly changing, and some people are finding it difficult to accept the way this has changed. However, even the expression of their reservations about the present or loyalty towards the older version of Nepali national identity shows that they do still keep themselves connected with the 'old' Nepal, revealing how different people associate differently with the sense of Nepali identity.

This chapter illustrated the close relationship between ethnicity and roots in the study of nations and nationalism. I stated that travel and tourism can have immense effect in enriching and reinforcing 'root' identity, especially to the diasporic communities who identify with their cultural origin importantly tied to the idea of their nativeness. I have argued that strong association between homeland travel and its positive relation to enhanced root identity resonates with nationalism. This chapter suggested the potentials of the Nepali diasporas community evolving as a new market for Nepal's tourism sector. Unlike other forms of travel in which travel is primarily stimulated by visitors' curiosity to know new and interesting people or their pasts, the diasporic travellers are driven by a search for familiarisation and identification with others, and visitors seek personal enrichment through a sense of being 'at home'. Given the growing Nepali diasporic communities in recent years, it would be judicious for tourism administrators of Nepal to consider 'different' ways to entice Nepalis' diasporic communities in its tourism plan. In this case, the recently declared Visit Nepal 2020 could be a good start, as we have noticed that other countries have been using such national celebrations for similar purposes. Such endeavour could be meaningful not only in economic sense but also in forging stronger ties of diasporic community with the home nation and its culture, boosting a form of nationalism that would become increasingly pertinent for Nepal in future.

References

Adhikary, K. (2012). *Nepalis in the United Kingdom: An Overview*. Reading: Centre for Nepal Studies United Kingdom.
Al-Ali, N. and Khoser, K. (2002). *New Approaches to Migration? Transnational Communities and the Transformation of Home*. London: Routledge.
Anderson, B. (1992). *Long-Distance Nationalism: World Capitalism and the Rise of Identity Politics*. Amsterdam: Centre for Asian Studies Amsterdam.
Antonsich, M. (2010). Searching for Belonging: An Analytical Framework. *Geography Compass*, 4(6), 644–659.
The Asia Foundation. (2015). *Aid Recovery in Post-Earthquake in Nepal: Independent Impacts and Recovery Monitoring Phase 1*. Kathmandu: The Asia Foundation.
Baldassar, L. (1997). Home and Away: Migration, Return and 'Transnational' Identity. *Communal/Plural*, 5, 230–249.
Barth, F. (1981). Ethnic Groups and Boundaries. In *Process and Form in Social Life: Selected Essays of Fredrik Barth: Volume* (pp. 198–227). London: Routledge and Kegan Paul.
Basu, P. (2007). *Highland Homecomings: Genealogy and Heritage Tourism in the Scottish Diaspora*. London: Routledge.
Bess, K., Fisher, A., Sonn, C. and Bishop, B. (2002). *Psychological Sense of Community: Theory, Research, and Application*. New York: Plenum Publishers.
Bhandari, K. (2013). Imagining the Scottish Nation: Tourism and Homeland Nationalism in Scotland. *Current Issues in Tourism*. DOI: 10.1080/13683500.2013.789005.
Billig, M. (2001). *Banal Nationalism*. London: Sage Publications.
Bista, D. B. (1999). *Fatalism and Development*. Patna: Orient Longman.
Boym, S. (2001). *The Future of Nostalgia*. New York: Basic Books.
Braziel, J. E. and Mannur, A. (2003). Nation, Migration, Globalisation: Points of Contention in Diaspora Studies. In J. E. Braziel and A. Mannur (Eds.), *Theorising Diaspora* (pp. 1–22). Oxford: Blackwell Publishing.
Brettell, C. (2006). Introduction: Global Spaces/Local Places: Transnationalism, Diaspora, and the Meaning of Home. *Identities*, 12(3), 327–334.
Brown, J. (2011). Expressions of Diasporic Belonging: The Divergent Emotional Geographies of Britain's Polish Communities. *Emotion, Space and Society*, 4, 229–237.
Brubaker, R. (1996). *Nationalism reframed: nationalism and the national question in the new Europe*. Cambridge: Cambridge University Press.

Brusle, T. (2012). Nepali Diasporic Websites: Signs and Conditions of a Diaspora in the Making. *Social Science Information*, 51(4), 593–610.

Carter, S. (2004). Mobilising Hrvatsko: Tourism and Politics in the Croatian Diaspora. In C. Tim and D. J. Timothy (Eds.), *Tourism Diasporas and Space* (pp. 188–201). London: Routledge.

Christou, A. (2011). Narrating Lives in Emotion: Embodiment, Belonginess and Displacement in Diasporic Spaces of Home and Return. *Emotion, Space and Society*, 4, 249–257.

Cohen, A. P. (1996). Personal Nationalism: A Scottish View of Some Rites, Rights, and Wrongs. *American Ethnologist*, 23(4), 802–815.

Coles, T. and Timothy, D. J. (2004). My Field Is the World' Conceptualising Diasporas, Travel and Tourism. In T. Coles and D. J. Timothy (Eds.), *Tourism Diasporas and Space* (pp. 1–29). London: Routledge.

Connerton, P. (1989). *How Societies Remember*. Cambridge: Cambridge University Press.

Datta, A. (2010). The Translocal City: Home and Belonging among East-European Migrants in London. In K. Brickell and A. Datta (Eds.), *Translocal Geographies: Spaces, Places, Connections* (pp. 10–27). London: Ashgate.

Duval, D. T. (2004). Conceptualising Return Visits: A Transnational Perspective. In T. Coles and D. J. Timothy (Eds.), *Tourism Diasporas and Space* (pp. 50–61). London: Routledge.

Gale, T. (2009). Urban Beaches, Virtual Worlds and 'the End of Tourism'. *Mobilities*, 4(1), 119–138.

Gellner, D. (2013). Warriors, Workers, Traders, and Peasants: The Nepali/Gorkhali Diaspora since the Nineteenth Century. In D. Washbrook and J. Chatterjee (Eds.), *Routledge Handbook of South Asian Diasporas* (pp. 136–150). London and New York: Routledge.

Gellner, D. (2015). Associational Profusion and Multiple Belonging: Diaspora Nepali in the UK. In N. Sigona, A. Gamlen, G. Liberatore and H. Neveu Kringelbach (Eds.), *Diasporas Reimagined: Spaces, Practices and Belonging*. Oxford: Oxford Diasporas Programme.

Harper, M. (2003). *Adventurers and Exiles: The Great Scottish Exodus*. London: Profile Books.

Hausner, S. and Gellner, D. N. (2012). Category of Practice as Two Aspects of Religion: The Case of Nepalis in Britain. *Journal of American Academy of Religion*, 80(4), 971–997.

Hollinshead, K. (1998). Tourism and Restless Peoples: A Dialectical Inspection of Bhabha's Halfway Populations. *Tourism, Culture & Communication*, 1(1), 49–77.

Hughes, H. and Allen, D. (2010). Holidays of the Irish Diaspora: The Pull of the 'Homeland'? *Current Issues in Tourism*, 13(1), 1–19.

Hutt, M. (1998). Going to Mughlan: Nepali Literary Representations of Migration to India and Bhutan. *South Asia Research*, 18, 195–214.

Kelly, M. E. (2000). Ethnic Pilgrimages: Peoples of Lithuanian Descent in Lithuania. *Sociological Spectrum*, 20(1), 65–91.

Larsen, J. (2008). De-exoticizing Tourist Travel: Everyday Life and Sociality on the Move. *Leisure Studies*, 27(1), 21–34.

Leite, N. (2005). Travels to an Ancestral Past: On Diasporic Tourism, Embodied Memory, and Identity. *Antropologicas*, 9, 273–302.

Lowenthal, D. (1995). *The Past Is a Foreign Country*. Cambridge: Cambridge University Press.

Malkki, L. (1992). National Geographic: The Rooting of Peoples and the Territorialisation of National Identity among Scholars and Refugees. *Cultural Anthropology*, 7(1), 24–44.

Marschall, S. (2012a). Tourism and Memory. *Annals of Tourism Research*, 39(4), 2216–2219.

Marschall, S. (2012b). Personal Memory Tourism and a Wider Exploration of the Tourism-Memory Nexus. *Journal of Tourism and Cultural Change*, 10(4), 321–335.

Marschall, S. (2015). Touring Memories of the Erased City: Memory, Tourism and Notions of Home. *Tourism Geographies*, 17(3), 332–349.

Mensah, I. (2015). The Roots Tourism Experience of Diaspora Africans: A Focus on the Cape Coast and Elmina Castles. *Journal of Heritage Tourism*. DOI: 10.1080/1743873X.2014.990974.

Morgan, N., Pritchard, A. and Pride, R. (2002). Marketing to the Welsh Diaspora: The Appeal to Hiraeth and Homecoming. *Journal of Vacation Marketing*, 9(1), 69–80.

Mulligan, A. N. (2002). A Forgotten 'Greater Ireland': The Transatlantic Development of Irish Nationalism. *Scottish Geographical Journal*, 118(3), 219–234.

Nash, C. (2002). Genealogical Identities. *Environment and Planning D: Society and Space*, 20(1), 27–52.

National Planning Commission. (2015). *Post Disaster Needs Assessment Executive Summary*. Kathmandu: Government of Nepal.

Nowicka, M. (2007). Mobile Locations: Construction of Home in a Group of Mobile Transnational Professionals. *Global Networks*, 7(1), 69–86.

Pariyar, M., Shrestha, B. G. and Gellner, D. (2014). Rights and a Sense of Belonging: Two Contrasting Nepali Diaspora Communities. In J. Pfaff-Czarnecka and G. Toffin (Eds.), *Facing Globalisation in the Himalayas: Belonging and the Politics of the Self* (pp. 134–158). New Delhi: Sage Publications.

Ralph, D. and Staeheli, L. A. (2011). Home and Migration: Mobilities, Belonging and Identities. *Geography Compass*, 5(7), 517–530.

Rauniyar, D. (2015). *Samsmaran, Bhukanpapachi America Dekhi Nepal Samma*. Available at: www.onlinekhabar.com/2015/06/285942/.

Schiller, N. G. and Fouron, G. (2002). Long-Distance Nationalism Defined. In J. Vincent (Ed.), *The Anthropology of Politics* (pp. 356–365). Oxford: Blackwell Publishing.

Sheffer, G. (1986). A New Field of Study: Modern Diasporas in International Politics. In *Modern Diasporas in International Politics* (pp. 1–15). London: Croom Helm.

Sheller, M. and Urry, J. (2004). *Tourism Mobilities: Places to Play, Places in Play*. London: Routledge.

Siwakoti, S. L. (2015). *Tan Americama Bhayepani Man Nepalmai Ghumirahancha*. Available at: http://global.setopati.com/america/713/.

Smith, A. D. (1991). *National Identity*. London: Penguin.

Subba, T. B. (2008). Living the Nepali Diaspora in India: An Autobiographical Essay. *Zeitschrift fur Ethnologie*, 133(2), 213–232.

TAAN. (2009). *Send Home A Friend Campaign to Run Till 2010.* Available at: www.taan.org.np/news/755-send-home-a-friend-campaign-to-run-till-2010.

Timothy, D. J. (2008). Genealogical Mobility: Tourism and the Search for a Personal Past. In D. J. Timothy and K. G. Jeanne (Eds.), *Geography and Genealogy: Locating Personal Pasts* (pp. 115–136). Aldershot: Ashgate.

Timothy, D. J. and Coles, T. (2004). Tourism and Diasporas: Current Issues and Future Opportunities. In T. Coles and D. T. Timothy (Eds.), *Tourism Diasporas and Space* (pp. 291–297). London: Routledge.

Urry, J. (1996). How Societies Remember the Past. In S. Macdonald and G. Fyfe (Eds.), *Theorizing Museums* (pp. 45–65). Oxford: Blackwell Publishing.

Urry, J. (2000). *Sociology Beyond Societies: Mobilities for the Twenty-First Century.* London: Routledge.

Vathi, Z. and King, R. (2011). Return Visits to the Young Albanian Second Generation in Europe: Contrasting Themes and Comparative Host-Country Perspectives. *Mobilities*, 6(4), 503–518.

Wang, N. (1999). Rethinking Authenticity in Tourism Experience. *Annals of Tourism Research*, 26(2), 349–370.

Wright, A. S. (2009). Destination Ireland: An Ancestral and Emotional Connection for the American Tourist. *Journal of Tourism and Cultural Change*, 7(1), 22–33.

6 Conclusions

In this book, I have considered the aspects of nation and nationhood articulated in tourism and illustrated that both nationalism and tourism collaborate in the expression of nationhood and national identity. The book has suggested that an assemblage of images, emblems, and symbols of Nepali nationhood in various touristic settings is meaningful because they provide a venue for articulation of nation and its characters. The use of various icons and pointers of Nepali identity in touristic settings provides a great sense of collective identity that serves two functions: (a) internal ascription, that is, the construction of identity by citizens with the nation and (b) promotion of distinctive touristic identity through the assertion of national uniqueness and a distinction of the nation within the larger international community. In short, the mobilising of national markers in tourism help in defining who is a member of the community and who is a foreigner.

I have also argued that touristic expression of the Nepali nation observes the fundamental propositions of nationalist doctrine, in that it re-iterates national unity, autonomy, and uniqueness, all of which play a part in differentiating a nation from 'the Other'. Greenfeld (1995) notes that the definition of a nation is at least in part determined by the perceived place of the nation in relation to other nations but maintains the notion of the nation as a primarily self-defining group. I argued that the exchange of 'selfhood' and 'the Other' is not always overt; however, the myriad representations in touristic sites create emotions that are directly associated with the idea of nationalism and nationhood, especially to Nepali visitors, both within and outside Nepal, to whom visiting Nepal and touristic attractions reminds them of their selfhood vis-à-vis other nations.

This book has illustrated that representation in tourism is a medium through which the culture and identity of the Nepali nation have been asserted to reaffirm its authenticity and uniqueness. For example, during the formative years, tourism in Nepal largely followed the political course that put great emphasis on mountain imagery, though this was partly informed by commercial necessity. Tourism representations also characterised monarchy as a fulcrum of Nepali culture that fastened the fabric of social and cultural diversity: it reaffirmed Nepal's uniqueness as a country untouched by modernity and a society interdependent on its rich tradition and culture, primarily as a melting pot of Hindu and Buddhist cultural practices. This narrative emphasised the important place of monarchy in people's everyday culture, depicting it as an institution that everyone admired and cherished. For example, the use of words like 'mystical kingdom' or 'Himalayan Shangri-La' in tourism promotional media was intended to achieve the above goals. In order to maintain the above narrative, the representations of Nepal that did not comply with this image of Nepal were not given enough attention, despite their immense tourism potential. An example of this was the region of Terai, which has largely been absent in national tourism discourse.

The above exclusion is helpful in explaining the existing struggle by Terai-based political groups to establish the '*Madheshi*' identity in the national narrative of Nepal. The *Madheshi* movement is essentially a challenge to this perception that Nepali identity only comprises hill and mountain culture. The ontological position that Nepal refers only to hills and mountains and its people has stimulated the 'alleged' exclusion and discrimination against the people of the Terai region. This book sheds light on the exclusionary nature of Nepali national identity through tourism perspectives. It suggests that the excessive use of mountain imagery in tourism fails to appreciate Nepal's national diversity, further marginalising the excluded communities from the national imagination. The *Madheshi* movement is the political expression of the exclusion of place, culture, and heritage of *Madhesh* in various outlets of Nepal's national narrative. This book argues that tourism is one of the outlets of national expression, and by providing proportionate representation of all groups in tourism media, it can help to project positive and inclusive national imagery.

This book has also discussed how Lumbini has recently assumed greater significance in the Nepali national imagination. It has suggested that Lumbini occupies an important place in the national iconography of Nepal. Buddha stands tall as an icon of Nepali identity, and Lumbini is a strong symbol of Nepali collective identity. The strong opposition to the proposed development project at Lumbini was an indication and a reminder that Nepali national identification is not formed independently but is strongly informed by the nation's interaction with and perception of the external 'Other', mainly India, and to a lesser extent, China. This brings the strong presence of a geopolitical ingredient to the expression of Nepali nationalism; the conflict over Lumbini was an example of a perceived threat from geopolitical competition between India and China over Buddhist heritage in the region and a defence of Nepal's autonomy and authority over Gautama Buddha's heritage. The case also restated that national or international monuments and heritage sites are repositories of national identity and serve as resources for interpretation and articulation of the nation and its autonomy and freedom. Finally, I have presented some examples of how the act of travel and tourism encourages self-reflection and instils a strong sense of belonging to the nation. It has been argued that diasporic visitors recollect 'home' during or after their visit, and such recollections contribute to their homeland identity and sense of belonging to their home nation. The narratives of the Nepali diasporic community in the UK who visited Nepal following the devastating earthquake in April 2015 showed that the earthquake invited an unprecedented level of engagement of the Nepali diasporic community with their home nation, providing a setting for the expression of feelings and show of love for the country, which is associated with the idea of homeland nationalism.

All of the above cases advanced the idea that tourism is a form of collective interaction, and the various symbols, icons, and representations in tourism are driven towards maintaining the distinctions between the interacting groups. These representations make actors taking part in tourism conscious of their self-identity, and tourism acts as a place to ascertain the maintenance of a boundary with the 'Other' or the outsider. Barth (1981) suggests that the cultural features that signal the boundary may change over time; however, with greater interaction and exposure the cultural characteristics of the actors may likewise be transformed, and there is always a boundary between members and outsiders. It is interesting to note that cultural references to mark identity or boundary have changed in Nepal over the years, though it has been noted that the pace of change towards embracing social, cultural, and geographical diversity in tourism representations has not been very encouraging. The growing propensity of the Nepali middle-class population to travel and the marked growth expected in international visitors to Nepal means that the narrative of Nepal will find newer ways to distinguish itself from 'the Other', creating a stronger border in the future.

The arguments in the book closely correspond with Lanfant (1995), who takes the view that tourist products and the state exploit the tourist image to reinforce national identity. She also notes that the mobilisation of tourism in 'nation flattering' is more organised in countries which have recently acquired political independence, which are experiencing movements for regional autonomy. Given Nepal's historical political change in the recent years, there are examples of similar practices in the new federal structure of the Nepali state. At the national level, the wider role of tourism has been recognised in the new Constitution that has appreciated the need for identifying, protecting, promoting, and publicising the historical, cultural, religious, archaeological, and natural heritage sites of the country and prioritising local people in the distribution of benefits of the tourism industry. The Ministry of Tourism and Civil Aviation has started preparing a detailed project report to develop one model tourist destination in each of the seven provinces. Similarly, in order to bring regional balance to tourism activities and boost the overall tourism industry, it has also initiated a process to identify the top 100 travel destinations throughout the country. At the provincial level, the newly formed provincial governments have started to collect data of local and provincial attractions to exploit them more effectively through tourism.

In the above context, the book has wider relevance, as it can open up new areas for the exploitation of local resources and heritage in tourism and help us understand tourism's wider role. Scholars of tourism have viewed touristic culture as socially constructed through discourse (Pritchard and Morgan, 2001; Aitchison, 1999). Franklin and Crang (2001) note that touristic culture is more than physical travel; it is the preparation of people to see other places as objects of tourism and the preparation of those people and places to be seen. 'Local' people are now more exposed to the archaeologies of tourism – to more knowledge about their locality, their past, geography, economy, literature, nature, and so on, and this encourages a reflection of one's identity and belongingness to the place, within which the narrative of the nation finds a place. Additionally, this book opens a debate on the role of home travel in the expression of 'homeland' nationalism, an area that has been completely overlooked by scholars of the Nepali cultural world. Diasporas and other transnational actors can play a role in the development of a kind of nationalism, which is directed outward, across the boundaries of territory, and directed towards members of their own ethnic nationality. In this form, nationalism brings together those who share a sense of 'peoplehood' based on shared culture and history by situating people in their homeland.

This account will be useful in broadening our understanding of tourism beyond its economic significance. In many developing countries, discourse on tourism has largely remained focussed on the economic implication of a neo-liberal approach to the nation's overall development. In other cases this has been corrected, with some appreciation of its role in heritage preservation, conservation, or environmental protection. The important place of tourism in fostering greater national unity and strengthening the sense of belonging and identification with one's nation has largely remained absent in scholarship. Additionally, in the case of Nepal, scholarship of nationalism has largely focussed to a great extent on caste, ethnicity, and religion, and the important role of other sociological objects such as leisure, travel, and tourism is largely absent. It is hoped this book initiates a debate to fill this gap. In terms of practical implications, the book provides a useful insight to tourism managers in Nepal into appreciating the mobilisation of tourism for a creative and positive self-image of the country.

In conclusion, the book urges us to look into the power of tourism to influence identity, to assert one's distinctiveness, and to create a difference between 'us' and 'them' and in particular the way a national story is presented through touristic objects to showcase a nation's uniqueness, distinctiveness, and the asserting of nationhood in Nepal. However, such discussions could benefit more if they included a perspective from international visitors and how they interpret these representations and markers of identity in touristic settings. Future studies could include the readings of heritage and iconography from such international visitors. Additionally, considering the challenging character of the Nepali state, it would be useful for scholars from various other disciplines to see the intersection between nationalism and national identity from their disciplinary platform: for example, geographers could study the role of landscape in the construction and expression of Nepali national identity. I hope this book will inspire other scholars to open such debates in future.

References

Aitchison, C. (1999). Heritage and Nationalism: Gender and the Performance of Power. In D. Crouch (Ed.), *Leisure/Tourism Geographies* (pp. 59–73). London: Routledge.

Barth, F. (1981). Ethnic Groups and Boundaries. In *Process and Form in Social Life: Selected Essays of Fredrik Barth: Volume* (pp. 198–227). London: Routledge and Kegan Paul.

Franklin, A. and Crang, M. (2001). The Trouble with Travel and Tourism Theory. *Tourist Studies*, 1(1), 5–22.

Greenfeld, L. (1995). Nationalism in Western and Eastern Europe Compared. In S. E. Hanson and W. Spohn (Eds.), *Can Europe Work? Germany & the Reconstruction of Postcommunist Societies* (pp. 15–23). Seattle: University of Washington Press.

Lanfant, M. F. (1995). Introduction. In M. F. Lanfant, J. B. Allcock and E. M. Bruner (Eds.), *International Tourism: Identity and Change* (pp. 1–23). London: Sage Publications.

Pritchard, A. and Morgan, N. J. (2001). Culture Identity and Tourism Representation: Marketing Cymru or Wales? *Tourism Management*, 22(2), 167–179.

Index

Printed in the United States
by Baker & Taylor Publisher Services